BLACK BOOTS AND SHORT TROUSERS

(A Personal Memoir of Life in a Boys' Home in the 1940s)

by
SYD SHARP

ISBN 0 9525281 0 X
© Syd Sharp 1995. All rights reserved. No reproduction, copy or transmission may be made without written permission.
Typeset by Create Publishing Services Ltd
Printed & Bound by Redwood Books

ACKNOWLEDGEMENTS

It would not have been possible to have written this book without the help of others, mainly my wife, Lily Sharp, for the hours patiently spent typing and correcting the original handwritten manuscript. Mr. Alan Vincent and Mr. Ken Holland, the General Secretary and Accountant of Mr. Fegan's Homes for allowing me to search the cellar of Fegan's Homes' Head Office in Tunbridge Wells, for old photographs and magazines about the Homes. Mrs. Vivienne Knapman and Dr. Phil Pettit for their time spent in reading and suggesting corrections (and offering encouragement). Mrs. Margaret Brazell for her inspiration toward the title of this book. Mr. Peter Osborne for drawing the "Just William" character for the cover, and many others who have encouraged me to keep writing to the end. Also those who have kindly allowed me to quote them or to use their names. Should I have inadvertantly omitted to mention anyone, please accept my sincere apologies.

Syd Sharp

CONTENTS

CHAPTER	ONE	WELCOME TO YOUR NEW HOME	1
	TWO	JAMES WILLIAM CONDELL FEGAN	13
	THREE	SETTLING IN	29
	FOUR	THE UNCHANGEABLE ROUTINE	41
	FIVE	SUNDAY AND THE CHAPEL	53
	SIX	MR. GEORGE	63
	SEVEN	CHANGE AT LAST	73
	EIGHT	CAMPING IN KENT	91
	NINE	THE FARM	101
	TEN	OLD BOYS AND REUNIONS	127
	ELEVEN	CANADA	137
	TWELVE	FINALE	147

FOREWORD

For a number of years now, whenever I have related stories of my days as a boy in Mr. Fegan's Homes either to my colleagues where I was employed or at talks given to various organisations i.e. Churches, Chapels, Schools and even an Archealogical Society, someone has invariably said to me "you should write a book".

I did attempt this a few years ago but gave it up as I found it too traumatic re-living my early days.

Then having retired, I decided to try again. Shortly after I had begun again a lady wrote to me and said that her father was in Fegan's Homes at Stony Stratford for two years from 1934 and was then transferred to the Training Farm at Goudhurst. She went on to say "The picture given by booklets/articles I have seen of Fegan's Homes contrasts immensely with the picture I got from how he used to speak of it that was when it was mentioned at all . . . I suppose what I'd really like to know is what it was really like. As a Fegan boy yourself I'm hoping you might be able to tell me, from your own personal experience, what it was like – if you feel you can, of course, and don't mind".

So I wrote back to the lady in question and said that I was writing a book and putting down my experiences.

I have tried hard to avoid exaggerating the hard and tough side of those days nor to paint too rosy a picture of the good days, and there were some (especially at the Training Farm).

This book will never be a polished work of literature, and is not intended to be one. It is a simple record of my life as a boy, some of it spent in a Boys' Home.

I trust that, apart from being of interest to many, it will also answer the question put to me by that lady who wrote the letter saying "I suppose what I'd really like to know is what it was really like".

If you really want to know read on, for only an old Fegan Boy can tell you that.

Syd Sharp

*I WEPT BECAUSE I HAD NO SHOES
UNTIL I MET A MAN WHO HAD NO FEET.*
Chinese Proverb.

Chapter One

Welcome to Your New Home

It was early March 1944. Had you been passing through the small town of Stony Stratford in North Buckinghamshire, situated on the A.5. – the Watling Street that ran from London to North Wales, you may have noticed three boys looking up at the grey stone walls of what was then Mr. Fegans Homes for Boys, the Orphanage to the locals, and in the background a voice was saying "Welcome to your new home". They, the locals, were the fortunate ones. They were going home to their friends and their loved ones and their familiar surroundings.

We, Bert, Ronnie and myself had said goodbye to our friends, most of whom we would never see again, and our relatives, who we would not see for many years to come. Then the door in the wall was opened and we went in and became Fegan Boys.

Home for me had been Enfield, where I had lived with my Grandmother, until she died. My Grandmother was a Saint, although, to my knowledge, she never went to Church, but the sacrifices she made to look after me, and the way she looked after me, put her in that category as far as I'm concerned, and I only wished she had lived longer so that I could show in some way my gratitude for all that she did for me. But then, had she lived, I wouldn't be writing this story.

Following Grandma's death I went to live at Chalk Farm, near Camden Town, with my Auntie. The air-raid siren was at the end of the road, and at night we lay in bed and heard the people running down to the Underground Station, which was also at the end of the road. We didn't go down there as my Auntie said it wasn't healthy, and so we lay in bed listening to the guns, and the bombs. The houses on the opposite side of the Street had already been hit, leaving nothing but rubble and a short cut to school (Haverstock Hill School) when nobody was looking.

One of my memories of the days spent at Chalk Farm were the happy hours I spent on Hampstead Heath. The Londoners did not call it 'Appy Ampstead' for nothing! Even during the war wonderful Fairs were held there, with all the roundabouts, dodgem cars, coconut shies, whelk stalls etc. You name it and it was there.

I loved feeding the ducks on the large ponds there, but I think what attracted me more than anything else was the Barrage Balloon that was kept flying by the R.A.F. personnel, mainly the W.A.A.Fs. Any Reader not familiar with those days may be interested to know that these massive gas filled Balloons – with a tail shaped very much like the tail of an aeroplane – flew above London (there were hundreds of them) and were kept from floating away by a very strong cable about half an inch in diameter. It was this cable that deterred the German aircraft, that bombed London so badly in the earlier years of the War, from low flying, as these cables were capable of causing an aircraft to crash.

I spent hours watching the Balloon being raised and lowered by a mechanical winch driven from the rear of an R.A.F. lorry. It never lost it's fascination for me, whether it was, what seemed like, miles up in the sky or on the ground sometimes being cleaned by the ladies in the W.A.A.Fs.

I well remember one hot summers day, running down a gravel path to go and have a swim at the nearby Lido, wearing only a pair of swimming trunks and plimsoles. I tripped and slid full length along the gravel path. It took a piece of skin from off of my hip, about the size of a 50p. piece, and grazed the whole of one side of my chest. My Auntie, who was with me at the time, not knowing quite what to do, took me to one of the huts that the R.A.F. personnel who looked after the Barrage Balloon lived in. One of the men gently held me down and another emptied about half a bottle of Iodine over my chest and hip. Before starting to do this he said "Sorry, this is going to hurt", and was he right! To this day, I still have a scar on my hip, but having been bandaged up by these gentlemen I was grateful for their help, although there were many painful days to follow. I still get a nostalgic feeling when I see a Barrage Balloon.

It was, of course, here on Parliament Hill Fields where those in the ill-fated Gun Powder Plot with Guy Fawkes sat and watched hoping to see the explosion when the Houses of Parliament were blown up, as not only Westminster but a great area of London could be seen from that vantage point. As a boy, I often sat there (maybe on the very spot!) and looked across at this fantastic view, the main focal point being St. Paul's Cathedral.

We then moved on to Bounds Green in North London, to escape the German bombing. I remember the day we moved because I felt very privileged to travel in the cab with the driver of the removal van. As we approached Bounds Green, quite near to the house we were moving into, there was a great crowd of people looking down the railway embankment. When I asked the driver what they were looking at, he said "Oh, the Germans dropped a bomb there last night." I cannot remember how long I lived at Bounds Green with my Auntie, and her four year old Son, but they were very happy days indeed.

I attended Bounds Green School that was opposite the Underground Station, and it was a very friendly School, including both Staff and Pupils. The School boasted a full Orchestra, which played regularly for morning Assembly. In reply to an invitation to those who wished to join the Orchestra I went along and took the test for the Violin. The Music Master who conducted the test told me that he would play two different notes on the Violin and he would then play one of those notes again. I was to tell him which one of the two he had repeated. Alas, they all sounded the same to me, so I guessed – and guessed wrongly. On reflection, maybe if I had been honest and confessed that they all sounded the same I may have fared better. This was the beginning, and the end, of my musical career.

Most Saturdays in the Winter found me down at White Hart Lane, the home of Tottenham Hotspur Football Club. It was only a tuppenny bus ride away.

The entrance fee was eight pence for boys and two pence for a programme – and a further two pence for the return journey. The whole outing coming to one shilling and two pence in old money or approximately 7p in today's currency. It was wartime and, as Arsenal's ground had been taken over by the Government, they shared White Hart Lane with Tottenham, which meant that there was a game every Saturday of the Season. I had many happy afternoons at the ground, sometimes with 40,000 or more in the crowd. The first game that I saw was Tottenham against Chelsea and Tottenham won 5–1. And, for some reason which I could not explain to anybody, I then decided to become a long-suffering Chelsea supporter, and have remained so for the rest of my life. I still believe that, somehow, I made the right decision. In that game I saw a player who had become famous for an outstanding feat (still in the record books) of scoring ten goals in one game, when he played for Luton Town; his name was Joe Payne. I saw many other famous players including Cliff Bastin, Ted Drake and – probably one of the finest full-backs I have ever seen in my life – Eddie Hapgood, as well as Tommy Lawton, the England centre-forward who played for Aldershot whilst being in the Army. Most of the players were in the Armed Forces at the time and were Sergeants, and above, in rank, and some were Officers, such as Flight Lieutenant Bernard Joy.

During the summer I spent most of my spare time in the recreation ground at Bounds Green, which was just about a road away from where I lived. I played a lot of cricket and was fortunate enough to play for the School in a few matches against other Schools. Two or three roads away, in the opposite direction to the recreation ground, was Alexandra Palace. Often I used to play or walk in its grounds and one day, throwing a tennis ball up at the wall of the Palace, it stuck under the arm of a Statue, and a nearby workman with a ladder, retrieved it for me. When he gave it back he said, "There you are son, if you can do it again I'll give you ten shillings." Ten shillings was a lot of money in those days, but I was grateful to get my ball back and decided not to bother. It is strange how small incidents like this remain with you for the rest of your life.

But, alas, it seems that this happy carefree life that I had discovered was not to last. My Auntie was expecting another baby and her Husband, who had been serving as an Officer in the Army overseas, was returning to this country. It seemed that there just wasn't room in the house for me as well. So I was told that I was going to "another school" where I would live-in. It sounded almost as though it was a Public School. Of course, I would come home for holidays; of course there was a lovely swimming pool, but there wasn't a swimming pool at Stony Stratford, neither did we go home for holidays, and had I known the real truth, who knows, I may have made a run for it. But where did a boy, just turned twelve years of age, run to in those days anyhow?

And so I said goodbye to all my friends at Bounds Green School, and some of the Staff, and, although I didn't realise it, I would never see them again.

When I had been at Fegan's for two or three months a parcel arrived for me and it seems that my old friends in my class in Bounds Green School had had a collection for me and with the proceeds the School Mistress had purchased three books, and she had sent them to me, together with an individual letter from every one in the Class. I cried as I read the letters and it only made me even unhappier than before to think of all my old friends who were still living a normal life. I still have those books to this day. Every boy in the Home had to write a monthly letter in School, so I used mine to write to say "Thank you" and I have never forgotten the kindness of my old friends at Bounds Green.

And so, on that fateful morning, 2nd March, 1944, I travelled with my Auntie to the Head Office of Mr. Fegan's Homes for Boys, which was situated at 64 Horseferry Road, Westminster, and there I was given a short test by Mr. Walmsley (Uncle Bill to all Fegan Boys). The questions were very easy:

1. Name all the positions on a Football field. (I had not been going to Tottenham all this time for nothing!)

2. If oranges were 2d. each, how much would 6 cost?

I managed to do this and it seems, on the strength of this test, and because of my physical fitness, I was accepted by Fegans Homes.

Later, one day when I was scrubbing the notorious tiled passage that ran the 240 yard length of the Home at Stony Stratford, I thought "You weren't very smart Syd Sharp, you should have answered the questions incorrectly and maybe they would have failed you" – although I have never met another Fegan Boy who was asked any questions before entry. So, I had failed the music exam at Bounds Green and passed the entrance exam to Fegan's Homes. How stupid can one get?

So, I said goodbye to my Auntie. I did not know it then, but it would be at least seven years before I saw her again. So Bert, Ronnie and I were then taken by the Superintendent and Matron of the Home at Stony Stratford to the Station at Euston and then by train to Wolverton. When I lived at Chalk Farm I often stood on the Railway Bridge over the rails that ran from Euston to the North and looked up the line, wondering where it went to. Looking back it almost seemed as though a finger of fate was pointing and saying "That's the way".

The Green Van

And so, after a journey that I wish to forget, we arrived at Wolverton Station and were met by a green van with "Mr. Fegan's Homes Incorporated" stamped on the side. We got into the back of it for the two or three miles' journey to Stony Stratford, and we became Fegan Boys.

Having had nothing to eat all day, we were taken to the kitchen, but I cannot remember whether we ate or drank anything. We did not feel like eating or drinking. Suddenly, what had happened had caught up with us and had become a reality – and it was too late to do anything about it.

Bert could not stand it any longer and he began to cry and I unashamedly joined in. The cook, at that time a lady, turned us out of the kitchen. She said she could not put up with us crying. So we were let loose among 180 other boys, with their constant questioning – "What's your name?" "Where do you come from?" "Can you play football and cricket?" "Can you fight?" and so on. All we wanted to do was to creep away somewhere and lose ourselves.

It was bath-night at Fegan's. Boys were running around in boots and no socks on. These were tied around their legs, ready to be handed in for the laundry basket. Later on I was to be initiated into the task of sewing these dirty socks together. 180 pairs of them. The reason being to keep them in pairs, as each sock had it's owner's number on it. A group of boys would gather in the room by the laundry basket and untie the knots in the socks ready for them to be sewn together. One of the ladies in the workroom, where all the clothes were repaired and sorted, would be in charge with needles and thread. Using double cotton, we put five stitches in each pair. She then cut the cotton and we sewed the next pair. Whilst this was being done, she would constantly chant "Come on boys, five stitches, double cotton, speed up, speed up". There weren't many jobs that we did not have to do at Fegans.

Then a Housemaster appeared on the playground and blew a whistle. The moment the whistle was blown everybody had to stop. If you were chasing a football you stopped as soon as you possibly could. Sometimes, if someone was accused of moving, then they were called forward and found a job to do; so everybody stopped. A voice then said "One to fifty, come and get your bath." Everybody had a number in Fegans. The number was on your socks and on all of your clothes; even stamped on your boots. I was No. 73. And so it went on – another blow on the whistle "Fifty to a hundred, come and get your bath" and later on "A hundred to hundred and fifty, come and get your bath", and then "the rest, come and get your bath". Bert, Ronnie and I ignored all of this, but we were rounded up at the end. Despite protesting that we had already had a bath that day, we were given another bath. Nobody was exempt from rules at Fegan's Homes.

And so, probably one of the worst days of my life was coming to a close.

I was shown to a bed and given a nightshirt that reached to the floor. There were no pyjamas in Fegan's in those days. We hung our shirts and socks over the bed-rail at the foot of the bed and put the rest of our clothes in a wooden box at the side of our bed. Then we had to kneel and say our prayers. My only prayer was to go home. We then got into bed and silence reigned.

Talking after lights-out was not allowed, nor getting out of bed. Any offender, if caught, was punished quite often by being strapped. I don't remember whether I slept that night. It seemed a strange and awful nightmare to me. In the morning, for a brief moment, I thought maybe I had dreamt it. Perhaps it wasn't true, and I was going back to school with all the others at Bounds Green. But it was true, and somehow life would never be quite the same again.

Reveille in Fegan's was 6.30 Nobody was called twice. Everyone went down to the large bathroom and stripped to the waist. After washing, we were lined up and inspected by the Housemaster. Hands, wrists, elbows, face, neck and knees were inspected. We always washed knees at the same time. If he didn't think you were clean enough, or you had not washed properly, you were sent back to wash again, and, if necessary, again. If you passed, you then gave your number to a boy who stood by him with a marking-off board. No. 73, and he put a tick by your number. Nobody escaped washing.

Strip wash in the Bathroom.

Everybody had a job. Some did it before breakfast, some after. The playground was swept every morning before breakfast, except for Sundays, rainy days and Christmas Day. It was never dirty. There was never any paper on it. Sometimes I felt it was the same dust pushed backward and forward down through the years, but it had to be done.

I have never in my life been fussy about food, but breakfast at Fegan's was very basic. Two slices of bread, about half an inch thick, with a thin layer of margarine on, and porridge. It took a long time to serve everybody. The serving of breakfast was done in complete silence, and the porridge was not very warm, nor was the cocoa. Fegan's cocoa was an education to drink!

One morning of each week (I believe it was Tuesday) we arrived in the Dining Hall to find the cups on the table were half to three-quarters filled with salts. Not those nice fizzy ones I had previously taken when I had been ill or recommended by a Doctor, but these tasted like nothing I had experienced before. There was no way of getting out of drinking this foul-tasting stuff; anyone who tried was given another full cup to drink. Try as you may it was impossible to drink it in one gulp, so you always had to take another go at it. What the reason was for this added torture to everyday life, nobody seems to know. Then, to add insult to injury, we had to drink our cocoa out of the same cup, without it having been washed out. After breakfast came the inevitable jobs, washing-up, scrubbing, polishing, etc. etc. Fegan boys scrubbed everything, and there was a lot of area in Fegans to be scrubbed. If 'A' levels had been given for scrubbing most Fegan boys would have gone to University. After this, everyone went into the boot-room, which was next to the bathroom, and boots were polished. Everyone then made himself tidy and ready for school.

School was upstairs. Fegan's ran it's own School with five classes. They packed every boy into one class for morning assembly and prayers – no Orchestra playing! This wasn't Bounds Green. If only my old friends at Bounds Green could have just come and had a peep I'm sure they wouldn't have believed it. School wasn't as high a standard, academically, as Bounds Green. I cannot remember whether I learnt anything or not in those first few months. It's doubtful. You cannot feel completely disorientated, rejected or unhappy and at the same time become a good scholar.

The Headmaster, "Dad Swell", was a pretty good sort. Six foot four and no nonsense. Most Fegan boys liked "Dad", as they called him. He stood no nonsense, for discipline seemed to be the order of the day everywhere. "Dad" used to conduct the Choir on Sunday night in the Chapel. Providing you could read – words, not music – you were in "Dad's" Choir, and Dad did the rest. In fact, the boys had a little poem. It went like this:

> Mr. Swell is a very good man,
> He goes to Church on Sunday,
> He asks the Lord to give him strength
> To cane the boys on Monday.

At breaktime during the morning session of school on Monday, we had to walk through Dad's class to go downstairs. All the Choir would give him a quick glance, and anyone who had misbehaved, by Dad's standard, on Sunday night was told to stand by the screen, where Dad would read the Riot Act to him and persistent offenders found that the poem was true.

By now, they had taken away my nice blue shirt, my shoes and other clothes, which I took for granted at Bounds Green, and replaced them with a Fegan's grey shirt, navy-blue polo-neck pullover, a pair of trousers, jacket, pair of socks and, of course, boots. Everyone wore boots. Boots with studs in. Two boys had the job of boot-studding, and there was a regulation number of studs allocated for each boot. I forget how many it was, and only the really big lads, and those with influence with the boot-studders, had more studs in their boots. You could tell a boy's standing by the number of studs in his boots. Sometimes it meant he was a bully; sometimes it meant he was genuinely a popular lad, a good footballer or cricketer or something like that.

So, in two or three days, the change was complete and we now looked like everybody else.

Front Entrance at Stony Stratford: Note roof damaged by Fire on the 30th March 1938.

Lots of boys in Fegan's, especially new boys, would tell you that they weren't going to be there very long. A relative or somebody or other that they knew was going to come and collect them and take them away, and occasionally that actually happened, yet somehow I knew in my heart that this was not going to happen to me. Maybe the Reader will feel that I've painted a grim picture of those early days in Fegan's Homes, but I am only writing the truth, as it actually happened. Fegan's Homes in Stony Stratford in those days was a grim place to me. A member of the Staff told me, years later, that a man, who visited the Homes whilst I was there, told him that he couldn't sleep for a week or more afterwards, thinking about it. Fortunately, and I wished I had known this then, things were going to change, and change for the better, but that is later in the story.

Believed to be the first boys at the Stony Stratford Home 1900–1901.

Chapter Two

James William Condell Fegan

When I first went to the Home at Stony Stratford I often stood looking at the large picture of Mr. Fegan that hung in the Dining Hall. Sometimes I would stand there for twenty minutes to half an hour not just because I was so moved by the picture but because it gave me a chance to be on my own, and looking at it did not attract any unwanted notice. Getting time on your own wasn't very easy with 180 other boys around, not to mention Staff.

So Mr. Fegan gazed down at me with what I thought was a kindly face and I wondered when he would put in an appearance, and if he did perhaps he would speak to me and give me some reassurance about the future, which looked so bleak to me. Strangely enough, I had never really worried about the future before but now I was desperately unhappy and I just wanted a way to escape from the nightmare that Fegan's Homes was to me in those early days.

Well, Mr. Fegan did not put in an appearance, so one day I asked another boy when Mr. Fegan would be coming to Stony Stratford and was promptly informed that he wouldn't be coming because he was dead. I later found out that he had died in 1925 – before I was born.

Mr. Fegan was born on the 27th April 1852 and was the youngest of four children born to Anne and James Fegan, of the Ordinance Survey Office in Southampton. Until he was 10 years old he was educated by his Mother, who incidentally lived until the age of 98. When he was 13, in 1865, he entered the City of London School, whose Headmaster was the famous Dr. E. A. Abbott. He gave Mr. Fegan a glowing report when he left the School in 1869. It is interesting to note that the Head Boy of the School at

Mr. J. W. C. Fegan. The Picture I studied when I first arrived in 1944.

that time was one named H. H. ASQUITH, who was later to become the Prime Minister of Britain.

In 1870 he went to work for a firm of Colonial Brokers in the City (Mincing Lane). Life was not all work and no play for the young Fegan. Like myself, he had a great love for football and cricket, but his Mother, fearing that he was getting too fond of football, steered his interest towards art. However, it seems his real love was fishing, most of which was done in Ireland. He once laid claim to the British Isles' record for a day's sea angling with a rod and line, by catching about 1,200 lb of fish (including a Skate 147 lb.). This was in 1907 at Ballycotton, Co. Cork.

In the same year that he started work, (1870) whilst reading his Bible alone at home one evening, he felt that God was speaking to him and he committed his life to His Service, and shortly afterwards opened his first Ragged School in the evenings, in a very similar way to the famous Dr. Barnardo.

Mr. Fegan in 1891–39 years of age.

In September 1871, whilst convalescing in Bognor following a break down in his health, he found his first boy on the beach there, and took him back to London with him. A few years ago, an old Fegan's boy named Les Nicholas from Littlehampton built a block of flats near the sea front at Bognor and has erected a plaque there to mark the approximate spot.

In 1872, with the help of friends, Mr. Fegan opened his first Home for Homeless boys in Deptford. It was an industrial Home, designed to give training to boys, so that they might afterwards be able to earn a decent living.

In one of his magazines, Mr. Fegan told of one of his first boys. He related that there loomed up before him the dull, animal face of the boy that came into his first Home the day it was opened in 1872. He explained that he shrank from hurting a boy's feelings or lowering his self-respect by parading his former wretchedness. He was one of three forlorn street-arabs who lived by what they could pick up in the day, slept at night up a narrow cul-de-sac by the side of a dog-biscuit factory, for the sake of the glow of heat the ovens sent up to the flagstones above. They came to his Ragged School one night and begged to be allowed to sleep by the fire, as, although the flagstones were warm, there was no protection from the pouring rain. He let them sleep in the attic of his first cottage, and they were thankful to lie through the winter on the bare boards. Why did he not make them more comfortable? Because, if he had done so, he would have been besieged by a horde of other homeless waifs, and his Ragged School efforts would have been swamped.

W. Y. Fullerton, in his book J. W. C. Fegan, published in the 1930s, says that some of the boys taken in by Mr. Fegan in Deptford "were so disreputable and filthy, through sleeping in empty houses, cart-sheds and similar places, that they were actually ashamed to come even to the Ragged School."

It seems that they were Shoe-blacks, Match-sellers, Mud-larks, who grubbed in the river at low tide to make a living by picking up such trifles as they found there. There were boys from the Indigo factory nearby, blue from head

The first Fegan boy admitted to the Home in Deptford on the day of it's opening in 1872.

to heel, and costermongers, who raucous voices proclaimed their calling, and all claimed sympathy and help.

The demand soon became so great that the house next door was purchased and added to the Home, and Mr.

Fegan was now known as Fegan of Deptford.

In 1879, there were so many boys that The Little Wanderers Home was established in Greenwich.

The Little Wanderers Home, Greenwich.

It was about this time that Mr. Fegan's parents had moved home to Downe, in Kent, and "the Governor", as his boys and others now called him, spent as much time as he could spare with them in 1880 and then with his widowed Mother from 1881 to 1883.

During the summer he took his boys there for holidays, and so became the pioneer of camps for boys.

During their first stay at Downe they visited the home of Charles Darwin, who lived nearby, and they sang hymns in front of his house. Mr. Darwin expressed his sympathy with the work being done, by giving each boy sixpence and he received hearty cheers from the boys as they departed.

Mr. Fegan daringly asked Mr. Darwin if he might borrow his Reading Room, which he had established for the Villagers, (but was seldom used by them) to hold some Gospel services in. On a further request to use the Rooms to hold a Gospel Mission, he received the following letter from the great man:-

"Dear Mr. Fegan,

You ought not to have to write to me for permission to use the Reading Room. You have far more right to it than we have, for your services have done more for the Village in a few months than all our efforts for many years. We have never been able to reclaim a drunkard, but through your services I do not know that there is a drunkard left in the Village.

Now may I have the pleasure of handing the Reading Room over to you? Perhaps, if we should want it some night for a special purpose, you will be good enough to let us use it.

Yours sincerely,
Charles Darwin."

The Reading Room, then renamed the Gospel Room, held services for half a century, to great effect.

So Mr. Fegan, like George Muller in Bristol, Thomas John Barnardo in Stepney, William Quarrier in Scotland, Leonard K. Shaw in Manchester, J. B. Stephenson for the Wesleyans and C. H. Spurgeon was not only deeply involved in a rescue work for homeless boys but also much concerned with evangelism and the spiritual needs of his fellow men and women.

On the 31st July 1882 Mr. Fegan moved his charges to premises in Southwark, as the Lease had expired on the premises in Deptford, and there he carried on his work for some 30 years.

It is worthy of mention that round about this time Mr. Fegan, who was still working in his career in the City, was warned by his Doctor that he could no longer have two occupations and one would have to go or else he was in danger of a complete break-down of his health. So, not surprisingly to those who knew him, he resigned his business career and devoted his life full time to the rescue and training of boys.

And so it was, night after night, that he went out into the streets of London, often at two in the morning, with a lantern in his hand, looking for homeless boys in need of care and affection.

The Orphanage, Southwark.

Many are the stories recalled about these days, and the understanding that was shown to boys who, not used to an ordered and disciplined life, often ran away and were not punished but shown love and understanding, as they were trained and taught to make their way in the world in later life.

In the Southwark Home, which had six floors, a hundred and fifty boys at a time could be housed and taught a useful trade. There was a time when the intake was so great that additional premises had to be rented in a nearby Street.

None of this work was subsidised by the Government of the day, who, seemingly, closed their eyes to the problem of the great need of literally thousands of boys and girls of this country who struggled to exist and many of whom died for the need of the bare necessities of life such as shelter and a place to sleep and enough food to nourish their growing bodies. Much criticism has been hurled at our Churches and Christian Organisations down through the years, but here was just one great work that was able to provide for the help of so many boys by the voluntary giving of generous gifts by so many caring people from the

Churches, Chapels and humble Mission Halls of that day.

Some of the boys, who were taken in to Mr. Fegan's Homes in those days, were of course by the very nature of their previous life, frail and in need of fresh air and healthy surroundings. So a year after opening the Home in Southwark a smaller Home was opened in Ramsgate for the least robust, and those of doubtful health. This was in the year 1883.

In 1884, Lord Blantyre persuaded Mr. Fegan to make his first trip to Canada with ten boys, and it seems that he was so pleased with what he saw that he hurried back to get 50 more boys out that summer, Lord Blantyre donating £500 to pay for the whole party.

It is interesting to see the list dictated by Mr. Fegan in 1925 of the items of equipment and the outfit he was then giving to his emigrant boys and the prices of that time.

1 Trunk	19.6	1 pair Braces	2.0
1 Overcoat	1. 16.0	3 Collars	1.6
2 Suits at 36/-	3. 12.0	2 Ties	1.6
1 pair Working Trousers	11.0	4 Handkerchiefs	2.3
2 pairs Boots at 12/6	1. 5.0	Garters, Laces, Studs and	
1 pair Slippers	6.3	Links	1.10
1 Suit Bluette Overalls	14.4	1 Hair Brush	1.9
1 Waterproof jacket	6.9	1 Clothes Brush	2.5
1 Jersey	7.6	1 Tooth Brush	7
1 Sunday Cap	3.6	1 Comb	9
1 Weekday Cap	1.6		
1 Earflap Cap	3.0	Books:	
1 Scarf	2.6	Bible	4.0
3 Shirts with collars	1. 1.0	A marked New Testament	9
1 Tunic Shirt	5.0	Grace and Truth	1.0
2 Suits underwear	10.0	Traveller's Guide	6
2 Nightshirts	10.0	Pilgrim's Progress	1.6
4 pairs Stockings & Socks	9.3	Hymn Book	3
		Stationery	2.0

Total cost per boy £14.8.11.

In 1889 Mr. Fegan married Miss Mary Pope and very little seems to be known of how they met and of her background previous to their meeting. Yet that she would be a real partner to him and was to have the same love and devotion to his work amongst boys was never to be in doubt.

It is, however, told of Mrs. Fegan that when the final arrangements for a group of boys were made for them to emigrate to Canada, she spent three hours taking the boys, one by one, aside into her little sitting room and having a quiet Motherly chat with them and then presenting each with a gift of a Bible that every boy received when he left the Homes.

Mrs. Mary Fegan.

With so many boys in London, Mr. Fegan began to enquire into the possibility of acquiring a Home in the country, where he might gather all his boys under one roof and also that they might benefit from the fresh air and the peacefulness of the countryside.

The Boys and Staff at Stony Stratford, November 1936.

Somebody turned his attention to a small town in North Buckinghamshire called Stony Stratford, where a School, built for the Sons of Gentlemen called St. Paul's College, was for sale for the princely sum of £45,000. This being the year 1900, one can imagine the immense sum this was, especially as Mr. Fegan didn't have any money at all.

However, it was suggested to Mr. Fegan that he offer a tenth of the asking price, which was £4,500, and to everyone's surprise it was accepted, provided it could be paid within two weeks.

He put the proposition to his helpers and those who worshipped in the Home Mission Hall in Southwark, and they accepted the challenge, setting a date for two weeks time, on the 25th June 1900, for a Praise and Thanksgiving Service. So much prayer was offered that on the night of the meeting the total that had been given was £4,491, just £9 short of the requirement. Mr. Fegan announced this to the meeting and an old gentleman, living in an almshouse nearby, slipped away, and on his return passed the following note up to the front:-

"The Lord has told me to make up the balance of the money – nine pounds.

Please accept the sum in the name of the Lord for all He has done for me.

Please do not say who it is." It proved to be the sum he had saved for his own burial. A short while ago, in the cellar of the offices of Mr. Fegan's Homes in Tunbridge Wells, I found a slide taken of the letter, written all those years ago, and I have a copy of it.

Having raised the money, through the help of his supporters, many of whom were not rich people, Mr. Fegan moved his boys from Southwark and Ramsgate to St. Paul's College, Stony Stratford, now the Orphanage, and the boys remained there for 60 years.

Continuing to send his boys to Canada, to begin a new life there, and seeing the possibilities of farm life in that country, in 1910, having been given a gift of £3,000 to buy some farm land, Mr. Fegan chose a spot about 3 miles from Goudhurst in Kent, near Curtisden Green, called High Hordon. He purchased approximately 86 acres of ground

> June 25th, 1900
>
> Dear Sir
> the Lord has told me to make up the Balance of the Money £9.0.0 — please accept the Sum in the name of the Lord for all He has done for me
>
> £9.0.0.
>
> Please dont say who it is.

Copy of Letter found in Fegan's Office Cellar.

where he built a Training Farm. With the additional purchase of more land he had a farm of approximately 346 acres, much of it for fruit farming.

Mr. Fegan then employed farm staff and insisted that each one was an expert at one particular skill i.e. Sheep, Dairy, Horses, Fruit etc. Canadian equipment was then purchased and he even built a Canadian-type barn and thus he was able to send his boys to Canada fully trained,

Aerial view of the Boys Home at Stony Stratford.

The rear view of the Home at Stony Stratford, showing the kitchen gardens.

not only as farmers, but also familiar with Canadian equipment.

Inevitably not all boys stayed in Farming. Some found their way into Universities and became teachers, and at least one was known to become a broadcaster. One eventually owned a fleet of buses in Toronto and others entered many other trades and businesses.

It should be said here that most boys who went to Canada sent back to the old Homes enough money to make it possible for another boy to go out there and have the opportunity to make a fresh start in a new country. All those who contributed in this way had their names placed on the Roll of Honour, an immense board with the boys' names written in "round copper plate" which was added to yearly by a Sign-writer. Two of these boards hung in the Dining Hall at Stony Stratford and two in the recreation hall at the Farm at Goudhurst. It is believed that there were nearly two thousand names on the Roll of Honour. This was apart from the many other generous gifts that were contributed to the Homes by grateful old boys, such as paying for the cost of a bed for a boy in the Homes. In 1929 gifts were made to purchase two handsome oak bookcases to house the boys' library at Goudhurst.

It now became necessary to extend the Goudhurst Home for the boys on the Farm, and having extended the Chapel, Mr. Fegan, in the last year of his life, although a very sick man, was still planning, watching closely and advising day by day in the course of the erection of the new building. He had his heart set upon seeing it's completion before his death. But this was not to be and he did not live to see the crowning effort of his life-work finished. On the 9th December 1925 he passed away peacefully at Blantyre Lodge, Goudhurst.

After his death some of his Old Boys placed a plaque in the entrance to the Goudhurst Chapel, which read:-

"They that turn many to righteousness shall shine as the stars for ever." Many years later a young Syd Sharp used to stand and read this, when he had the job of giving out the Hymn Books to the visitors to the Farm Chapel on a Sunday evening.

Following the death of Mr. Fegan, Mrs. Fegan then took up the reins of the work, backed by the members of the

The Plaque in the Chapel at Goudhurst erected by the Old Fegan Boys.

Council, until one fateful night during World War II, the night of the 7th-8th October 1943, when a German Bomber jettisoned it's bombs, while being harried by a British fighter-plane. All the bombs, except one, landed harmlessly in the nearby fields. That one landed on Myrtle Cottage, killing both Mrs. Fegan and her niece Mrs. Keays, who was living with her. Both were buried in the same grave as Mr. Fegan, in the cemetery at Goudhurst. Thus ended an era of work amongst boys, started all those years ago in 1872 by "The Governor".

However, the Homes continued, and, although many changes would occur, still hundreds of boys and girls, including myself, were still to benefit from the selfless life of devotion and love given so freely by Mr. and Mrs. Fegan.

Boys in the 1950s viewing grave at Goudhurst of Mr. and Mrs. Fegan and Mrs. Lovell-Keays.

Chapter Three

Settling In

If you can force your heart and nerve and sinew
To serve your turn long after they are gone
And so hold on when there is nothing in you
Except the will which says to them 'hold on'
Rudyard Kipling.

Even after all these years, I still find it difficult when recalling those early months at Stony Stratford; both Bert and I found it very hard to settle in, and no amount of writing or talking can really convey to the reader the true depths of our feelings. Ronnie, who also arrived with Bert and myself on the same day at Stony Stratford, although also unhappy with his new surroundings, seemed to settle in much easier than us. He was much younger and I would have liked to have helped him, but really it would have been the blind leading the blind. Although he didn't know it then, he was not destined to stay in Fegans for very long and one day was taken away by a relative or friend. I often wondered what happened to him. He was very good at drawing pictures and I hope that he found a happier life, where he could draw undisturbed and produce many pictures of quality for the pleasure of others.

So, we became part of the system that was Fegan's Homes in Stony Stratford in those days, and the routine didn't change from week to week or year to year. In fact, having talked to some of the old Fegan boys, who were there years before me, it seems that the routine in 1944 differed very little from that in the 1920s. Change was a very nasty word in those days, and, although I wasn't aware of it at the time, I understand now that most things were judged by the criterion of whether the Governor (Mr.

Fegan) would have liked it or not and it seems that Mrs. Fegan wanted things to remain much as they were.

One day, Bert drew me aside and quietly confided in me that he was going to run away. It was classed as "doing a bunk" in Fegan language. He invited me to join him, and it's hard to say, even now, why I turned down the offer. Perhaps I lacked the courage, but probably the main reason was that I knew in my heart that, even if I made it back to Bounds Green, I should only have been sent back to Fegan's, and life was difficult enough as it was without the punishment that usually followed when a boy was returned to the Home either by a well-meaning member of the public or by the Police – who usually treated the boys with much understanding and kindness and who would have been horrified to have known the punishment handed out to the offender, on his return.

So, one morning, shortly after telling me of his intention, the boys in Bert's dormitory woke up to find his bed empty, and a strange excitement went round the building as the word was passed around that "the new kid had done a bunk".

Usually, on these occasions, the longer a boy stayed away without being caught, the stories of his whereabouts and exploits became more exaggerated, such as "He's jumped on a passing lorry going to London" or "He's got as far as Birmingham". Not that many of us knew where Birmingham was.

Sometime during the next day Bert reappeared, having been returned by the local Police, and it seems that he escaped the usual punishment, as he was a new boy. He also escaped it on his next trip over the wall, but on a third occasion, having once more been brought back, Bert was strapped on his bare buttocks by the Superintendent. This, as usual, took place in the Dispensary, where most punishment was administered. He then shaved off all of Bert's hair, leaving a very small piece at the front in the shape of a V (one could only assume to make him look silly). Then, for a reason that still cannot really be understood, he gave him a spoonful of castor oil.

Bert was then put into Defaulters, which meant that he

stood for all meals at the back of the Dining Hall, with his back to the other boys, and received dry bread for breakfast and tea with no second-course for the mid-day meal. He spent his spare time scrubbing floors, and, of course, would receive no pocket money on Saturday. The time spent in Defaulters was usually one week, although I have known it last longer, and pocket money would not be restored for a number of weeks. One does wonder what would have happened if Bert had done something really wrong? He wasn't allowed to write home and tell them what had happened, as all letters were read by the Staff before being posted, and, even in those days, many people would have found it hard to believe.

Many years later, after the Home at Stony Stratford was purchased by the Order of Franciscan Monks for a Preparatory School, I pointed out to the Headmaster of the School, the two window recesses where Bert and other Defaulters stood for their meals, and I said to him "You probably won't believe this", and when I had finished telling him about the hair-shaving and the dry bread, he said "I believe it, as you're the fourth old Fegan Boy to have told me about this, so far".

We now live in a more enlightened age, and much more would be done now to help a boy whose only crime was that he wanted to be with such friends and relations that he had in this world.

However, this brutal treatment of a boy, who just longed for love and understanding, did nothing to deter his determination to get away from Stony Stratford. One Sunday night, being fast asleep in bed, I was woken by one of the Schoolmasters, a Welshman, and as he shook me awake, he asked "where's—, boy?" using Bert's surname, and, of course, I told him I didn't know, which was the truth. For the first time, Bert had run away without telling me. It was a spur-of-the-moment decision after Chapel. Not that I would have told anyone, had I known. Eventually I managed to convince the Schoolmaster that I really did not know where he was, and he left me to go back to sleep. Much later, when it was dark, I was woken again by the same Master and he said "We've found—, boy" (again using Bert's surname) "And only three people know about this, and you are one of them. Nothing is to be said". He did not have to tell me that twice. It seems that the Schoolmaster, after having woken me the first time, went home on his bicycle (he lived in Wolverton, about two miles away) and just on a hunch, went to the Railway Station in Wolverton, and who should be sitting there, waiting for the next train to Euston, but Bert. The train was due in about five minutes, and I often wondered how far he would have managed to get had he caught it.

The Schoolmaster took Bert home with him, gave him a slap-up supper and tried to encourage him to face up to the problems of Fegans Homes. Then he brought him back and hushed up the whole affair. Strangely, Bert never ran away again. I never forgot the Welsh Schoolmaster, and would have done anything for him after this episode.

As time went by I began to settle down to the everyday routine of Fegan's Homes at Stony Stratford. It took about six months. Being summer was a help, as there was some very nice countryside in the area, although we did not go out very often. When we did, it was always in groups of about fifty, and we walked through the town two by two in a long crocodile. Being dressed all the same, and wearing boots, we looked very different to the local people, who stood and stared at us. It seems that we weren't allowed to speak to them and they certainly did not attempt to speak to us.

I used to look at them and think, 'a short while ago I was like them and had the freedom that they and I took for granted'. How I longed to change places with them.

One day, whilst out on a walk through the town, I suddenly recalled my days at Enfield, where often I would see the boys from a nearby Roman Catholic Orphanage walking out in a similar fashion. They looked very rough and tough to me, and I always felt uneasy when I saw them. Now, suddenly, I realised that I looked the same as they did, and it seemed that fate had caught up with me, and I knew exactly how they must have felt.

Boots became a problem, having never worn them before. I found that they rubbed the skin on my insteps where the laces were, and as the problem became worse I was given a pair of black sandals to wear until the blisters healed, and then I went back into boots. Years later, when the Royal Air Force issued me with a pair of boots, they proved no problem. In fact I found the R.A.F. to be a nice cushy ride after Fegan's Homes.

My love for football hadn't gone away, and, although at first I didn't feel like playing games of any sort, eventually I joined in some of them that we played on the playground with a tennis ball. I found that wearing my black sandals was ideal for these games but I think somebody decided that if I could kick a tennis ball about then I could wear boots, so back to the boots it was. A tennis ball was a very valuable commodity to us in those days, both for playing football and cricket. I believe that most of them were supplied by the Stony Stratford Tennis Club, whose courts backed on to our walled-in garden. The members kindly threw their old tennis balls over for us.

One of the problems with tennis balls was their persistent ability to get lodged in the gutters around the roof of the building, and many a boy took amazing risks, climbing up the drain pipes to the gutters, to retrieve a tennis ball, and, of course, there was the risk of being caught by a member of Staff and of the inevitable punishment.

The North Wing of the building had dormer windows, projecting out half way up the roof, so that, if you looked out, you looked down the roof to where it disappeared over the gutter, and, although it wasn't possible to see into this, it did seem rather close. One afternoon, when everyone was in the "Boot Room", cleaning up for school, Jimmy—tied a piece of string to one of the bed rails in the dormitory and hung the string out of the window. He then proceeded to climb out onto and down the roof to retrieve his tennis ball from the gutter. Half way down, he began to slide, the string slipped out of his hand and he slid over the gutter and landed 30 feet below, on to the playground. Another boy, who was keeping lookout for him, was able to raise the alarm and Jimmy was soon whisked off to Northampton Hospital (about 14 miles away) where at first they wouldn't believe the story, as not a bone in his

Fegan's Homes Football Team 1945 – Author is standing on the far right.

body was broken. He did however limp for a long time but made a full recovery, and later in life did his National Service in the Army.

The boys at Fegans were divided into Squads, which denoted their status and their pocket money. When a new boy arrived he was put in what was called 3rd Squad. The Squads went up to 1st and down to 5th and pocket money remained the same as it was in Mr. Fegan's day (who died in 1925). Here is a table of the Squads and their pocket money:-

1st Squad (Table Boy)*	6d.	3rd Squad	2d.
1st Squad	5d.	4th Squad	1d.
2nd Squad	4d.	5th Squad	Nothing.

Defaulters stood up for all meals, went without their Second-Course, had dry bread and were given extra work to do.

* A 1st Squad Table Boy sat on a stool at the end of one of the twelve tables in the Dining Hall and was responsible for the others sitting at his table, including supervising the return of plates and cutlery to the scullery, and pouring out the tea and cocoa for them.

When I first arrived at the Home the boys in 1st Squad wore red badges pinned to their jerseys and 2nd Squad boys wore blue badges.

Every Friday evening without fail, a ceremony called "Characters" was held, when it was decided what Squad a boy would be in. Most of the Staff would sit behind a table on the platform at the end of the Dining Hall, with the Superintendent in the centre. The boys whose numbers were 1–50 would line up and the first boy would walk up to the table, stand in front of the Superintendent, salute and say "No.1, 3rd Squad, Sir" (or whatever his Squad happened to be). The Superintendent would look over his glasses at him. His school marks for the week would be looked at and, provided none of the other Staff had anything to say, the Superintendent would say "3rd Squad" and the boy would say "Thankyou, Sir," salute and walk away. Then No.2 would take his place, and so on, until the last boy, who would be numbered between 150 and 200, was dealt with. Sometimes a boy went up a Squad, though it took a long time for this to happen. Sometimes a boy went down a Squad and some received lectures and warnings about their behaviour. Once a year, during the school holidays, "All-day Characters" was held – known to the boys as "Judgment Day".

The Dining Hall, Stony Stratford, 3rd May 1909.

I cannot remember if there was a fixed date for "All-day Characters", but it was always held during the Spring or Summer. It had been instigated by Mr. Fegan and, therefore, it had to go on at that time.

Every member of the Staff had to attend, except for the Cook and her assistant, who were females, a lady who worked in the Staff quarters and two ladies who worked in the sewing room. So, for one day of the year, the boys knew where every member of the Staff was – sitting round a table in the Dining Hall with the General Secretary of the Homes, at that time a Mr.H. Milner-Morris, there judging nearly two hundred boys. Boys appeared before them, ten at a time, starting, of course, with Nos 1 to 10.

A boy was detailed to blow the whistle to summon the next ten boys when it was their turn to appear, so that no member of the Staff had reason to leave the table. There was, of course, a break for lunch. The rest of the day couldn't have been arranged better by the boys themselves. For weeks before the big day boys were all asking each other "what are you going to do on Judgment Day?" It was unwritten law that an opportunity like this (when all of the Staff were occupied) could not be wasted, and boys, who were shut in for the rest of the year decided to make hay while the sun shone. Some made their way, via the sports field, to the local Recreation Ground, where they played on the swings, roundabouts, see-saws, or talked to the local girls, if they were there. It may not sound much, but this was a taste of freedom that was denied the boys every other day of the year. As for talking to girls, it would have given the Superintendent, and some of the Staff, a severe heart attack had they known.

Others went for a walk in the town, but not many, as there was always a risk of someone reporting them. Quite a few climbed the roofs and looked for tennis balls in the gutters. One lad, Douglas—walked round the part of the Chapel roof that protruded above the playground and threw down a number of tennis balls to boys waiting below.

Some actually climbed the Steeple, but made sure they kept away from the side that could be seen from the main road. I never saw any boy do this and really doubted that it actually happened until in the early 1950s, when the Steeple was taken down. The Builder, who carried out the work, told me that there were a number of boys' names written all over it, in different writing, so boys must have managed to climb it somehow.

Not every boy went off on an expedition or took to the hills, but a great many did, especially the older ones. Those who didn't enjoyed the luxury of being able to relax by themselves for one day of the year.

To my knowledge, in my time, not one boy was ever caught breaking the rules on Judgment Day and far more activities took place than I have related here.

I've often wondered the feeling a boy must have had when he had just been promoted to 1st Squad and told that he was making good progress (not causing any trouble) when he had just come down from writing his name on the Steeple!

One thing that I did in those early days that helped me to accept that I was now in Fegans to stay (at least until I was seventeen, which seemed a long way off) was to shut out of my mind Bounds Green, my Auntie, my old School and, of course, my Grandma. She had done so much to keep me from Boys Homes and Orphanages and would have been horrified had she known my situation.

I wasn't aware at first that I was closing my mind to the past, but as time went by it became easier, although there were rude reminders. Occasionally I received a letter from my Auntie, and once she sent me a fruit cake she had baked, (maybe she had found out what Fegan's food was like). Letters used to upset me, although I didn't tell anyone else, and the cake, for some strange reason, really made me very unhappy, although it was intended to do just the opposite.

I still kept my interest in football and tried telling the other boys about Spurs, Arsenal and Chelsea. This was one part of my past that I didn't close my mind to and I managed to cope quite well.

It wasn't possible to listen to the football results on a Saturday evening, as Fegans didn't allow us to listen to a

Radio, not even for the news, although it was war-time. The only time I ever heard the Radio was a couple of times when England played Scotland at football. For Saturday's results we had to wait until Monday when the daily newspaper was posted up on a board in the shed in the playground. Two copies of the paper, the Daily Graphic, were bought to do this. Sometimes there were pieces cut out, where it had been censored. I had taken an old scrap book into Fegan's with me, in which I used to stick pictures of footballers out of the newspapers. With an old dinner knife I often cut out the pictures from the Daily Graphic on the notice board. Sometimes, if, in my enthusiasm, I removed them before the other boys had read the paper, an argument would develop and I then had to try waiting, in the hope that nobody else would beat me to it, as one or two other boys took up collecting also. I cannot remember where the paste came from to stick the pictures in my scrapbook. My 2d. a week pocket money didn't go to buying glue or paste. Maybe one of the Housemasters helped out, as some of them were very kind and helpful indeed, and I got the impression that they did not all approve of the way things were run.

 I well remember one Sunday morning when the "House boy" (who waited on the table for the Staff meals, washed up, and even ate his meals there) slipped out of the front door early, and took a Sunday newspaper out of the letter-box of a house on the opposite side of the Street. Unfortunately, a lady who lived nearby saw him and reported the incident to the Superintendent, who then held an identification parade on the playground. Nearly two hundred boys lined up and the lady walked up and down looking at every boy. Strange though it may seem, only one boy was absent, and that was the boy who had stolen the paper. His duties as House boy made him exempt from parades. When the lady in question came to the last boy, rather than admit she couldn't recognise the boy she had seen, she told the Superintendent it was him. That particular boy had straight fair hair, the guilty boy had dark curly hair. You couldn't have found a greater contrast. However, when the boy who was picked out protested that it wasn't him, and somebody remembered that the House boy was absent, he was immediately sent for, and the lady then said "Yes, that's him". I have never had much faith in identification parades since then. The House boy lost his job, and, of course, the usual punishments followed.

It wasn't the absence of a Radio or other things, like reasonable food or even shoes, that I missed in those early days. It was the freedom to walk out on my own occasionally or to be able to confide my feelings to someone. I felt I was a person with rights as a human being, and should not be constantly punished for trivialities. I had become No.73 and was no longer Syd Sharp.

Many years later I met a man who told me that his father was in charge of one of William Quarrier's Homes in Scotland, and it seems that these boys were treated very much as we were in Fegan's Homes. He told me how he often said to his father "These boys have done nothing wrong Dad" but nobody seemed to take any notice.

Chapter Four

The Unchangeable Routine

No Institution could possibly run smoothly without those two ingredients "discipline" and "a daily routine". Most everyday families have a daily routine, however flexible it may be; a time to get out of bed in the morning, a time to leave for work etc. So why was the routine, the daily life of the Orphanage at Stony Stratford so different to, say, the average family or Public School or of the Services? I suppose the first answer is that, however tough a Public School might be, there were holidays and quite long breaks from the routine of the School, whereas nobody went home from Stony Stratford. It seemed that Fegan's now owned you – for better or for worse. As for comparison with the Armed Forces, when I was called up a year after leaving Fegan's to serve my two years' National Service in the Royal Air Force, it was like a holiday camp, after what I had been used to.

This was underlined by an old Fegan boy named Tom McClean, who served in the Paratroop Regiment and became famous for rowing the Atlantic Ocean single-handed. In his book 'Rough Passage' he said "Para Regiment training was like a kid's tea party after Fegan's, although you could not make some of the others believe that."

So what was it in those days that made us boys feel that we were prisoners? I suppose it was the lack of variety and the fact that one wasn't allowed to think for oneself. The old Army saying puts it 'you aren't here to think lad, but to do as you're told'.

Fegan's routine was as rigid as an iron girder. The moment you opened your eyes in the morning and realised that you were still there (and how often I longed to wake up at Bounds Green and find it had all been a nightmare?)

and then remembered what day it was, you knew exactly what would happen and what meals you would be eating.

Breakfast and tea didn't vary much in Fegan's. The bread for tea-time was spread by the boys at lunch-time, before going back to school. It was three slices per boy (two for the younger ones) one slice spread with marg and two with jam. The jam was spread on to dry bread, so you can imagine what it was like by tea-time. If you were lucky, you may have been given a crust instead of an ordinary slice of bread. This was served by a Master, who put the slices on your plate as you filed past him. The boys had their own language and a slice of bread was known as a 'nag' and a crust as a 'noggy'. One boy, let's say his name was Smith, one day did an Oliver Twist and said to the Superintendent who was serving out the bread that particular time "Please Sir, may I have a noggy" and to everyone's surprise he was given one. For ever after he was known as 'Noggy Smith'.

A rota of mid-day meals meant that they were the same every week. Monday – rissoles, Tuesday – stew (Cabbage stalk stew, we called it), Wednesday – Pease Pudding and so on. Once or twice a week, for the second course, we had "Baby heads". These were small puddings made in individual metal bowls, (one per boy and half for smaller boys). These were covered in treacle, which may sound great, but the treacle had been watered down, by adding boiling water, and was poured out of a jug. Fegan's treacle didn't stick to the spoon like everybody else's did, because it was too thin.

One day, when Baby Heads were about to be served, the Housemaster on duty realised that there was no jug with which to serve the treacle, so he said to the Dining Hall boy "Go and get me a jug". The boy quietly said "Go and get your own jug", thinking he could not be heard, but the Housemaster had heard him. He called him up to the platform and, holding him with one hand, he started hitting him with the other. The other boys' response to this was to call out "Good old Dave", which was the Christian name of the boy being punished, and gradually a chant went up of "Good old Dave". During a lull in the chanting the Master hit the boy again and said "Now say good old Dave". The boys, realised that if they did they were only going to make it worse for Dave, and they then went quiet. The Housemaster, now realising that he held the upper hand, once more challenged us to say "Good old Dave". In the silence that followed a lone deep voice from the Boiler Room, which was next to the Dining Hall, shouted "Good old Dave". The Boiler boy didn't go unpunished, but was a hero for many weeks to come, as far as we were concerned.

Sometimes for tea, we had fishcakes and these were really good and actually made with fish, whereas the rissoles were made of 90% bread and 10% meat. I may be generous with the meat percentage, as I once worked in the kitchen, and helped make them. Despite rationing, I could not believe how little meat there was in the mixture.

All the cooking was done in steam ovens in the Boiler Room. The boiler was kept stoked by one of the boys who had left school and was waiting to go to the Training Farm at Goudhurst. The food was cooked in large metal containers that were oblong in shape and had a handle at each end. They were made to fit the ovens, so there was only an inch between them and the oven walls. This made it very difficult moving the containers out of the oven, when everything was extremely hot. The boys called the containers 'coffins'. One day a boy was removing a 'coffin' from the top oven, which was chest high to him, and he accidently pulled the container of hot food all over his chest. As he was wearing only a shirt it scalded him very badly. In a panic, he ran to the sink and kept pouring cold water over himself. After having spent some time in the Sick Bay, the local Doctor pronounced him fit and said that "Despite doing all the wrong things, he had healed extremely well". We now know that what he did was the right treatment for burns. I've often wondered if the Doctor in question did not miss a chance to make a name for himself?

Reverting to the days routine, having been called at 6.30 a.m. everyone made his way to the bathroom for a strip wash. This was so called because we all stripped to the waist, removing a shirt and blue polo-necked pullover.

(Fegan boys didn't wear vests). Having washed and been inspected it was then time for breakfast, followed by 'jobs'. Some boys had already finished their particular task before breakfast, such as "parade sweeping". The playground at Fegan's was called the parade, as we paraded for meals, paraded for school and for a variety of other reasons, weather permitting, and I am given to understand that in Mr. Fegan's day, and for many years after his death, the boys were actually drilled, as in the Army. Some even had stripes sewn on to their coats and were given ranks. This was all intended to instill some discipline into them. Later the drilling was discontinued, but the discipline remained.

It would be far too lengthy to record all the different tasks that the boys were given to do, mostly to be completed before going to school, and only the very smallest boys were exempt from these.

Immediately after breakfast everyone made his own bed. This was done in a special way, with the blankets being tucked in at the bottom of the bed to produce a fold that was called 'pig's ears' and I well remember being hit by the boy in charge of the dormitory, on my first morning in Fegan's, for not making 'pig's ears', which I knew nothing about. Had I not been feeling so homesick at the time, I may well have hit him back, (which he deserved,) but I never forgot, and later, when I was a Senior Boy, I always helped new boys as much as I could. I still despise bullies. There were not many bullies in Fegan's, but those that there were I later discovered, to be, like bullies the world-over, abject cowards at heart, and there is no exception to this rule.

One of the jobs I was given was lining up the beds, and, of course, I had to wait for everyone to finish making their bed, and also for the boys who swept the dormitory to finish. Then, armed with a piece of string, provided by the Housemaster, I lined up the beds. Next to each bed was a wooden box with a lid, where each boy kept his Sunday Suit. These boxes acted as spacers, so that the distance between each bed was equal. I tied one end of the string to the third hole on the cast-iron frame of the bed at the end of the row and then took the string over all the beds and tied it to the corresponding hole on the bed at the other end of the row. I then turned back the sheets and tucked them in, so that they were in line with the string. Although this may not have been the intention, this meant that nearly 200 beds, in different dormitories, all had the top sheet turned down exactly the same distance as each other and in perfect line. A Brigade of Guards' Sergeant Major would have been proud of this! Some dormitories had three rows of beds, with as many as forty or more beds in them, and the centre row was not easy to line up. The other problem was making sure that nobody came into the dormitory and bumped into a bed until the job had been inspected, and your number had been ticked off.

Each morning the building was like a bee-hive for about an hour-and-a-half with boys everywhere scrubbing and polishing floors, cleaning toilets, polishing taps, cleaning basins, sweeping floors, collecting up soap, studding boots, washing up plates, knives, forks and spoons, etc. There were no teaspoons, thank goodness, and the cups did not have handles.

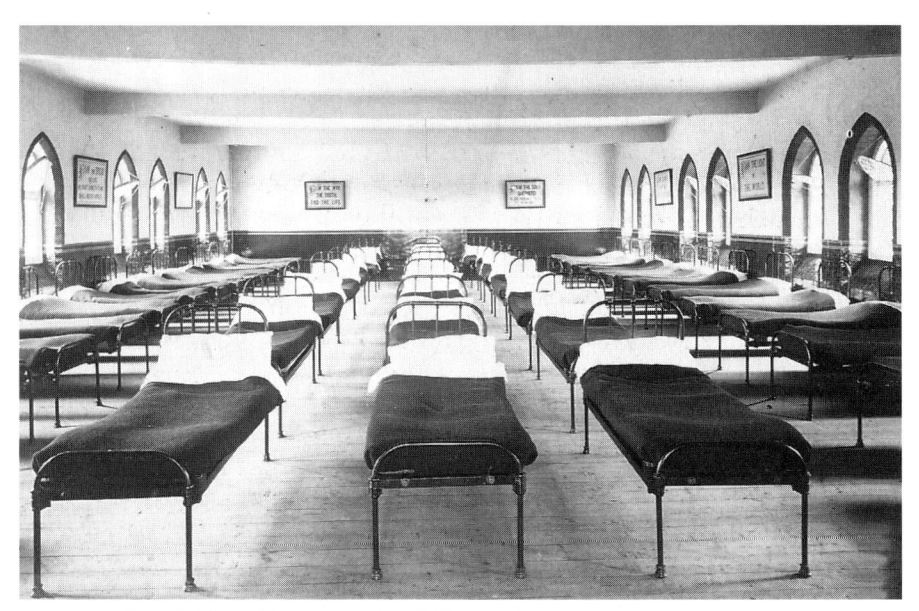

The North Wing Dormitory in 1920s.

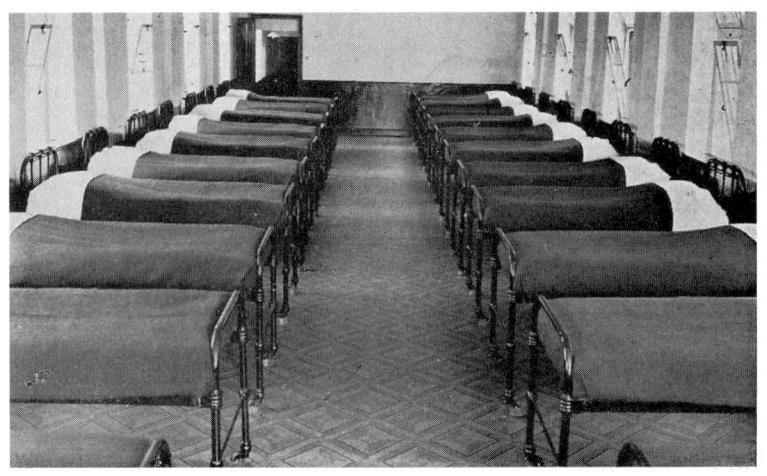

South Wing Dormitory 1950s. Note sheets in line.

Most of the equipment used for scrubbing, sweeping etc. was kept in a small room near the back yard, almost opposite the coke "dump". The room had no windows and was kept locked. Goodness knows why because no boy would go anywhere near it unless he had to do so. The place smelt, with all the damp floor cloths hanging in there. A boy was in charge of handing out the buckets, scrubbing brushes, brooms and floor cloths. So a queue of boys would form outside and one by one they asked for a bucket, scrubbing brush, soap and floor cloth. The boy in charge would write in the book provided, e.g. scrubbing set, and the boy's number; a boy on sweeping would ask for a B.H.D. (Broom, Hand Broom and Dustpan) and again it went into the book with his number alongside it. When the items were returned the boy in charge crossed out the item in his book and so it was ensured that everything was returned after use. There always seemed to be someone scrubbing, polishing or sweeping. In fact, some boys may as well have kept their scrubbing sets as they always seemed to be on punishment for some misdeed or other.

I was friendly with the boy who issued the kit and often went into the store with him and sat on an upturned bucket and had a chat. It was a nasty smelly place, but at least it was peaceful.

I well remember being on washing-up duty in what Fegan's called "the silver room". Here all of the cutlery was washed. Fegan's "silver" had a habit of going rusty and some of the dinner knives were like hack-saws.

On one particular day, whilst we were busy washing up, one of the boys had removed the brass cover from the light switch, which was threaded on and could easily be removed by hand. Having removed the cover, the boy in question then threw a damp tea towel over the switch, and waited for some poor unsuspecting boy to pick it up and get a 230v electric shock. It never occurred to us that it might kill someone. Most boys were wise to this particular prank, having been caught once or having been told about it by another boy. On this particular occasion, the damp tea towel hung over the switch, concealing it from view, waiting for a boy to get hold of it, when who should come in the door, to see that all was well, but the Superintendent! On his way out, wondering why a tea towel should be hanging on the wall, he reached out and picked it up. For once he was on the receiving end. When he had recovered . . . he hit all six of us, but we all agreed afterwards that it had been worth it. Needless to say, our experiments in electrocuting others ceased from that day on, but these were the incidents that broke the daily humdrum of the unchanging and often harsh routine.

Under the leg of each bed in the dormitories was a round block of wood, hollowed out for the leg to fit into. The idea was that these would prevent the bed-legs from damaging the highly polished lino in the dormitories. It doesn't take much imagination to realise that these blocks, called "pork pies" by the boys, were used in many different ways. Often a boy would get into his bed at night only to find two or three pork pies in it. I still have a scar on my forehead where it was split open when a boy threw a pork pie across the dormitory one night; although it was not his intention to hit me. He ended up in Defaulters. Sometimes boys threw them out of the window, at the chickens in the field that was alongside the Homes and often a boy would be detailed to take a bucket and go and collect up the pork pies from Mr. Toombs' field.

School at Fegan's was in the same building, only upstairs. We paraded at 9 a.m. and again at 2 p.m., having "cleaned up" which meant polishing boots, washing hands, combing hair and generally tidying up, and, of course, being inspected and marked off on the marking-off sheet. These sheets must have been sold to Fegan's by the thousand.

School was very much like any other school of that day, but for boys only. The Schoolmasters and one Mistress lived in the town or nearby and came in daily. There were five classes, and the Headmaster took the top class. Nobody sat the 11+ exam for the Grammer School, as at the age of 14 all boys left school and became working boys for six to eight months before going to the Training Farm at Goudhurst in Kent, where they stayed for about two and a half years.

Every day, after the younger boys had gone to school, the working boys, of whom there were about twelve to fifteen in number, did all the work that still needed to be done and that could not be handled by the school boys.

There were two boys who worked all day in the kitchen, and a boiler boy who carried the coke in by the barrow-load (which was also a job often given to a school boy as punishment). Another job was coke crushing. When the coke was delivered the pieces were too large for burning and had to be crushed by heavy weights on the end of long poles. A number of boys, as punishment for some minor offence or other, would lift the pole in the air, about two or three feet high, and then let it drop on to the large pieces of coke, which had been spread over the concrete floor, and so it went on – lift, drop . . . lift, drop . . . lift, drop . . . until the coke was crushed small enough. A boy once asked me, in all seriousness, if I thought they crushed coke in Hell. He was a tough lad, but even he did not fancy doing it for ever.

When I was there, one boiler boy fancied himself as an Engineer and one day managed to get a spanner from the Handyman's tools (without asking permission, of course). Then watched by one or two others, and the usual Fegan look-out, he undid a large bolt in the main plate of the hot water tank next to the boiler, to see what would happen.

Of course, what happened was that the bolt came out and flew past his right ear like a bullet, followed by a jet of very hot water. He, and the others, miraculously escaped, but the poor Handyman was soaked when he hammered a wooden plug into the bolt-hole. The coke boiler had to be raked out and then the hot water tank drained, before the bolt could be replaced. All this took about three days and we had to wash in cold water. The Staff kept saying "Blame . . ., the boiler boy, not us," but I had a sneaking feeling they delayed the repair just to rub in the lesson.

Another boy was appointed to look after the poultry – bantam chickens, although I believe the staff had the eggs. He also looked after the pigs.

The other working boys did gardening and various jobs that needed doing. There was also a staff boy who waited on the Staff at meal times and washed up their dirty dishes etc.

Weekdays were always the same, except for school holidays, when we amused ourselves mainly by playing cricket or football, with a tennis ball, on the playground. Some boys played Draughts or Chess. These sets were owned by Fegans and you had to ask to borrow them. Some boys read, but reading wasn't easy in Fegan's, as there wasn't anywhere quiet to read.

We also went for walks in the country and sometimes Schoolmasters came in and took us for walks. Occasionally we paddled or swam in a nearby river, but nobody went home.

On Saturdays there was often a football match in the sports field, sometimes against a team from the town or surrounding villages. When this was the case then everyone had to attend. I didnot mind as I liked both football and cricket, but hadn't yet made it into either of the first XIs.

Fegan's colours were black and red and this came about because an old Fegan boy W. W. Walmsley once played for the famous Black Heath Rugby Club and those were it's colours.

After one of these games of football, against a team from the town, I entered into conversation with one of the town players, and he said if he came to play us again he would

Cricket at Stony Stratford in 1930s.

bring me some comics. These were forbidden by Fegan's, but a few did the rounds, until they were confiscated. Sure enough, next time he arrived, he brought such a pile of comics that I could hardly carry them. But I was learning fast, and, having thanked him profusely, I smuggled them up to the dormitory and hid them in the box under my Sunday Suit, as the Staff seldom looked there. As I read one, I passed it on, and that too was passed on, and they kept us going for quite a while, and in some way it was a small victory for us. I smiled to myself whenever I saw a boy having his comic confiscated by a Master, as I knew there were plenty more where that had come from.

The opportunities to go out on ones own and without

Boating Pool in the back yard. Note coke dump in the background.

supervision were very rare, but on one occasion it was decided to send most of the older boys blackberry picking and we were divided into groups consisting of about 8 to 10 boys and given a very large jar. We were told that the group who picked the most blackberries would be given a prize of a fruit cake for tea. So away we went and at first picked as many blackberries as we could, but this unaccustomed freedom was too much for most of my group and they decided to go "scrumping" for apples. As I was only a 'new kid' I was detailed to stay and look after the jar and they would see me back at the Homes. So I sat on the bank of the canal and decided there was not much point in picking any more blackberries; for the first time I was on my own, enjoying the peace of the countryside. I also ate quite a lot of the blackberries we had picked. Later in the afternoon I walked back to the Homes, rather reluctantly, after the brief freedom that had so unexpectedly come my way.

I then made my way to the kitchen where others were handing in almost full jars of blackberries. Mine, which hadnot been very full even before I decided to eat some, was barely a quarter full. When I handed my jar in, the Matron said to me "You haven't picked many", so I said "They were difficult to find, Mum", and beat a hasty retreat. The rest of the group I had been with asked me if I thought we might win the cake. I told them it wasn't very likely as the other groups had picked so many.

There was another day for me that broke the routine and that was a visit from my Auntie. Not the one I lived with at Bounds Green, but another one who was single and serving in the W.A.A.F.s It was war-time, and being stationed at Cambridge, she wrote and asked if she might take me out for the day. This was allowed by the powers-that-be, but we had to be back in the evening. I do not know how many visits a prisoner in one of Her Majesty's prisons receives in a year, but in five years in Fegan's this was the only visit I ever received, and I was lucky, as most boys never received one.

Sometimes a boy would go out for the day and never return, but nothing was ever said by the Staff. It was just as though he had ceased to exist.

I well remember my day out. We went to Bedford by bus from Stony Stratford and after a lovely meal, went to the Pictures, to see Snow White and the Seven Dwarfs. By then I knew I only had a few hours of freedom left, and cried through most of the film.

After we came out of the Pictures, my Auntie put me on the bus to Stony Stratford and said goodbye. She told me to tell the Superintendent that she had left me at the bus stop, at Stony Stratford, which I did and he accepted my word not knowing I had travelled from Bedford on my own.

When I jumped off the bus at Stony Stratford, I walked down the High Street to the fish and chip shop, and, with some money my Auntie had given me, I bought a bag of chips and walked round the back way to Fegan's and ate them. I didn't care who saw me or reported me and I would have run away there and then but for the fact that I knew I would be letting my Auntie down. The next week or so was very difficult, and I felt just as upset as when I first arrived, so perhaps it was as well that it was the one and only visit I ever had.

Strangely, the next week at Characters, I was promoted to 2nd Squad, and the Superintendent told me that I had a very nice Auntie.

And so, it was back to the unchanging routine, but change, like the ocean tide, cannot be kept at bay for ever, and, although we didn't know it at the time, change was coming. The price to be paid was a costly one, for one boy at least in this country (not, may I say, a Fegan boy) but more of that later.

Chapter Five

Sunday And The Chapel

Sunday was different to every other day of the week at Fegan's, although all Sundays were the same as one another.

There was no floor scrubbing, dormitory polishing, parade sweeping nor many other major jobs that were an everyday part of our life the rest of the week. The boilers had to be kept going (but there was no coke-crushing). Although the regular kitchen boys were given the day off, two school boys were appointed to the work and were known as Sunday Kitchen Boys. Lots of other essential work was done, such as, washing up and laying out the tables in the Dining Hall. As there were no tablecloths, it was just cutlery. The plates were piled up on a table for the boys to pick one up as they went round to be served. Of course, the House Boys had to put in an appearance to wait on the Staff, but Fegan's had some very strict ideas about how a boy should spend Sunday.

After breakfast, having made your own bed (with pig's ears, of course), everyone changed into his Sunday Suit and placed his weekday clothes into the box at the side of his bed, which was very handy for those who had comics in the bottom of the box, as it covered them up, although Staff seldom looked in the boxes.

Our suits were made of some rather thick material that I believe was some kind of Worsted, and, although very difficult to put a crease in the trousers, it was very hard wearing. We also wore a grey shirt, a straight-sided black and red tie (that I have always referred to as a 'Just William' tie) together with the usual black socks and boots. Everybody wore short trousers, regardless of height. We had to wait until we were transferred to the Training Farm at Goudhurst until we could wear long trousers, and then everybody wore them. Fegans did like to make everyone look the same. Prior to my arrival at Stony Stratford, the boys wore dog collars (very much like an Eton collar) and there is no doubt that these were very uncomfortable to wear. I wonder why it was that Sunday, which was supposed to be a day of rest, always seemed to inflict upon us the burden of all manner of do's and don'ts, mostly don'ts. A more relaxed atmosphere would have been in keeping with the Gospel that was preached.

So we paraded for morning Chapel, with faces and hands scrubbed, boots polished and hair plastered down with Fegan's special brand of hair-oil, which was made up by the local Chemist. I often wondered what it was made from, but it was certainly not Brylcream, which was the No.1 hair cream in the outside world. The hair-oil was given out by a member of the Staff, from a huge bottle. He tipped a small amount into the palm of each boy's hand, as they lined up in front of him, which couldn't have been easy when the bottle was full.

One day the bottle was left unguarded on a table on the Dining Hall platform, so one of the boys jokingly shook it

Mrs. Fegan visiting the boys at Stony Stratford. (Black boots and Short Trousers).

over another boy's head, and the cork came out. It ran all over his head and down his neck, but other boys scooped up some of the surplus and put it on their own heads, and, with the aid of a towel, cleaned him up. Strangely enough, the Staff didn't seem to notice how much the level in the bottle had gone down. Hair-oil was only given out on a Sunday. The rest of the week we used water, although some boys did have hair-oil of various makes, sent to them by relatives and friends, in a 'parcel from home'.

Another small ritual was performed at this parade, before we actually went into Chapel, which was that the boys, who the previous day had donated a penny for the collection, were then given this same penny to place in the collection box themselves. It was against the rules to possess money, so it wasn't given out until the last moment. Maybe, the powers-that-be were afraid we may save up enough to buy a train ticket to London, or somewhere! However, it was only the first Squad boys who put a penny in the collection and this was mainly because of the belief that those who didn't, would not remain in 1st Squad for very long. It certainly was not unknown for the Superintendent, at that time, to quietly suggest to a boy that he ought to be considering putting a penny in the collection on Sunday.

We marched into Chapel, using a different entrance to the visitors who came in from the town and surrounding district. Many of the boys were in the Choir, facing the main congregation. The remainder of the boys sat at the front of the Chapel with the Staff, but never with the visitors. The Superintendent sat in front of the Choir, on a large chair facing the congregation. He always wore coat tails, a wing collar and a flower in his buttonhole. At the slightest noise from the choir he would turn round and glare at them, and that was enough of a warning.

The Chapel itself was a beautiful building, and had cost a considerable sum of money when it was built initially for St. Paul's College. The walls around the choir originally had some full-sized murals on them, mainly scenes from the life of St. Paul, and on the ceilings were paintings of stars and angels. However, Mr. Fegan didn't approve of all

The Chapel at Stony Stratford.

this, and had them painted over. He felt that the boys would be distracted by the pictures during the sermons that were preached during the Services.

One good thing about attending the Chapel was that for at least two hours every week (as there were two services on a Sunday) we saw ordinary everyday people, but, as in Kipling's "East and West", "Never the twain could meet".

I had never been to Church or Chapel before entering Fegan's Homes, although I have some vague recollection of going to a Sunday School when I lived at Enfield. We listened Sunday by Sunday to the visiting preachers who conducted the Services – London City Missionaries, Open-air Missionaries, China Inland Missionaries, 'Happy Jim' Bryant, whose face glowed and really loved the boys, Tom Rees, George Tryon (breezy George) E. G. Vine, George Woodall, the ex Buckingham Palace Guardsman and dance band pianist, known affectionately as "Uncle George" to all the boys, and many others from all walks of life who were probably the pick of the best preachers in the country and could not resist the invitation to address nearly two hundred boys plus a large congregation of people from the surrounding area.

If we ever had the chance to speak to a visiting preacher, before the service, we always asked him if he would tell us a story in Chapel. The boys loved stories, and some preachers did not need asking twice. They were only too willing to tell us many true stories about their previous lives. One told us of how he was a converted criminal and had been caught "by two angels in blue" (as he put it) whilst carrying a safe down the stairs of a building he had broken into. Years later, I was having my breakfast, and listening to the radio, when I heard a man telling the same story, and then I recognised the voice – it was the same ex-convict who spoke to us all those years ago in Fegan's Homes, and was still preaching the Gospel.

Whilst I accept that many things were done in the Stony Stratford Home that did not do credit to the message that was proclaimed on Sunday in the Chapel, it did not alter the fact that what was preached was the truth, and I believe that nearly all the Preachers who came to the

Chapel were very sincere men. Although we lived in what was then a harsh regime it did not alter the truth of the message that they preached or their teaching from the Word of God.

Meals were slightly better on a Sunday, and most Sundays we had meat for lunch and normally home-made custard for the second-course. In the summer the custard was made the day before, and placed on the floor of the massive fridge which was large enough to walk around in. The fridge was always kept locked by a large padlock and one day, when I was on Sunday kitchen duty, I had to put something in the fridge. So tucking the padlock under my arm, so that my hands were free to place the container on a shelf, I stretched out, and the lock slipped from under my arm into one of the large bowls of custard on the floor, that had now set like jelly. I decided the best thing to do was to roll up my sleeve and put my hand into the custard. I retrieved the padlock, leaving quite a large hole in the custard. To my amazement no questions were asked and the custard was served to the boys, so I decided to say nothing. I was learning fast.

If we thought that Sunday was a difficult day, then something was about to happen that even we could not have expected, and it made things one hundred per cent worse, yet really it was nobody's fault.

A new batch of grey shirts arrived. The old ones were handed in and the new ones were issued to every boy. It wasn't until we put them on that we realised that they made our skin itch quite badly, and the reason was some black hairy material mixed in with the grey. As we did not wear a vest or pants, the shirts were right next to our skin, and they really were uncomfortable and were soon known as "Itchy coos". Boys did everything they could to get rid of the black hairs in the material. Quite a few washed and scrubbed them, but it made no difference, and the laundering didn't alter things either. A few boys tried wearing their week-day shirt underneath, but once the Staff became wise to this, they went round checking that nobody had two shirts on. One member of the Staff said we were making a fuss about nothing and actually wore an

"Itchy coo" for a couple of Sundays, but it didn't last, and anyway, as the boys pointed out, he had a vest on underneath. So it was with great relief that we took our shirts off on Sunday night and were more than grateful that there was only one Sabbath in the week.

Although the evening service didn't start until 6.30 we all went to Chapel just before six o'clock where the Choir of sixty or more boys would sing Hymns and Choruses to the gathering congregation. The other boys attended also. People were attracted to the Chapel by the boys' singing and it was of a very high standard indeed. There always seemed to be at least one member of the Staff who was musically gifted and could either conduct or play the organ, often both. In my time Dad Swell, the Headmaster of the School, was the Choirmaster, and he was very popular with the boys. He took his singing very seriously, and, as many a boy found out, this was no time to play about.

Dad had a habit that we all felt would bring a catastrophe into the Service. When he brought the Choir to their feet, by raising his hand, he often pushed one of his feet against the marble rail that was behind him, in order to give himself a slight push off with his foot. This had the effect of rocking the marble rail on which stood two large vases of flowers. We all thought that one Sunday evening one of these vases would crash on to the steps below, but Dad said his prayers daily and the Lord must have been with him for not once did the flowers fall off.

Harvest Festival and Sunday School Anniversaries were good Sundays for us. Everyone loves a Harvest Thanksgiving, with all of the decorations, fruit, flowers and vegetables, and (with a Text on it) there was the largest loaf that I have ever seen.

So many people used to come that all the boys, who werenot in the Choir, had to sit in the transept at the side of the Chapel. We could not see what was going on, but neither could we be seen, and, although we behaved ourselves fairly well, it was nice to be able to relax from the gaze of 'Him who sat in front".

Sunday School Anniversaries were also very good, as the Sunday School was made up of children from the town, not Fegan Boys, and there were lots of girls of our age. Most of us were fed up with seeing only boys, but girls! they were a different matter.

The Sunday School sang in place of the Fegan boys' choir for that day. Very good it was too, but not one of us boys would concede that they sang as well as we did, which was a rather biased view, of course. The following Monday evening we all had to go back into the Chapel for the Sunday School Prizegiving. We entered into the spirit of the occasion by clapping and cheering those who received prizes and, of course, gave the loudest applause to the best looking girls.

(I had almost forgotten that I used to go to school with girls most days of my life.)

One lady in Stony Stratford told me some years later that when she was a girl she used to go to the Chapel at Fegan's just to see the boys, so we couldn't have looked so bad in our worsted suits and itchy coo shirts, but we only looked at one another and never had the opportunity to talk.

Looking back I do find it strange that the powers- that- be in those days kept the boys away from the people who lived in the town. In fact away from every other person except the Staff. Even the radio may as well not have been invented, as we never heard it. All decisions were made for us and then one day we were turned out into this world from which we had been cut off (in my case for five years and in other cases twelve years or more) and expected to handle it with ease. I marvel that so many boys did cope and made their way successfully.

I remember one morning after breakfast the deputy Superintendent asked how many boys could ride a bicycle, as he wanted a boy to deliver a message about two miles away. Only three boys put their hands up out of over 180 boys. How sad really. I was fortunate enough to be the boy chosen to do this errand and it was good to ride a bicycle again. When I was at Enfield my Uncle bought me a brand new bicycle. I often wondered what happened to it. I found out years later that somebody had removed the wheels and put them on to a truck they had made.

Some of the congregation in the Chapel in 1920s.

Most Sunday afternoons, weather permitting, we went for walks in groups of thirty or more. I was never quite sure if this was so that we could see the town or so that they could see us.

There were some very nice walks in the area then, as most fields had footpaths across them, and I suppose one of the favourites was across the fields to the Aquaduct, where the Grand Union Canal crossed the River Ouse in a metal trunk, known as the Iron Trunk to the locals. I have since read that the barge owners didn't like crossing it as they were suspended very high up, with literally nothing either side of them, and windy weather made them even more nervous, as the barge pulling at least one other behind it was buffetted into the metal sides of the Trunk.

It is interesting that it was mentioned by Lord Haw Haw (William Joyce) in one of his broadcasts from Germany during the war, when he said they would bomb it. It would have taken some hitting as it was so narrow. Of course, this didn't worry the boys in Fegan's Homes as they weren't allowed to listen to the radio and so didn't know about this threat to one of their favourite walks. I only found out about this in later years.

I can remember two other things that made Sunday different. One was that we had a slice of cake for tea (this meant no jam on our bread).

The other was that we also had a cup of milk before going to bed. There was no such thing as supper any other day of the week, except, of course, for the Staff.

And so to bed, when everyone, with great relief, removed their grey shirts. I suppose it was something like removing a pair of shoes that do not fit very well or haven't been broken in. The strange thing was that our weekday shirts were quite comfortable. I know some of the old Biblical Kings used to lament in sack-cloth and ashes. Those grey Sunday shirts were the equivalent!

Then it was back to Monday morning and the same unchanging routine. They say there isn't anything that lasts for ever and even Fegan's routine was about to change considerably.

Chapter Six

Mr. George

He stood on the raised Dining Hall platform, was of average height, immaculate but not over-dressed, not a hair of his greying head out of place, a serious looking man who could, when the occasion warranted it, break into a broad smile that led you to believe that he approved of any indiscretion that you had been involved in. Nothing could be farther from the truth. This ex-Indian Army Sergeant was one of the old school, and, although not brutal, was an absolute disciplinarian. So, when he announced that 'The boy wasn't born that he couldn't handle', we knew that either he or we would have to climb down, and although Fegan Boys were pretty tough, I have to confess, it was us.

Mr. George, as we called him, was the new Deputy Superintendent. So something was changing, even if it was only the Staff. Very little surprised us but this was very different indeed, as we were to find out. His surname, strangely enough, was the same as the Superintendent, so, to avoid confusion, we were told to call him "Mr. George" (his Christian name) never George and, of course, "Sir".

At first, he was shepherded around and shown the ropes by another member of the Staff, but a man like this did not take long to get the idea of how things were run, and the first day that he faced about one hundred and fifty boys on his own came during the school holidays. Having paraded for breakfast, on this particular morning, we filed into the Dining Hall, where he blew his whistle (very much like a referee's whistle). Whenever it was blown, one stopped whatever one was doing and kept quiet. The result was always immediate silence, unless you fancied doing coke crushing, or some other task that was crying out to be done.

On this particular morning, the first on his own, Mr. George decided that we had taken too long to become silent and so, without raising his voice, he told a boy to open the side door of the Dining Hall that led on to the playground (the parade) and then he quietly ordered us to file out and start running round the parade.

After a few laps I began to realise that this was going to last for quite a long while (it turned out to be about half an hour). So I slowed down to wait for a friend of mine to catch me up, thinking I could run round with him and exchange the odd comment about the situation, but what I didn't know was that 'the new chap' was sending everyone, whom he didn't think was running fast enough, to run up and down the garden path, which was wide and very long. Sure enough, he spotted me and I joined the twenty or so other boys who were running up and down the garden path. Any on-looker must have thought it quite a sight with over 100 boys running round the parade in studded boots, and another twenty or so running up and down the garden path.

After some time he stopped the boys on the path and put each boy's number into his notebook. (We were going to learn a lot about that notebook in the future). Then he told them to rejoin the others who were still running round the parade. Eventually he opened the Dining Hall door and we all filed back into breakfast, and were served cold porridge, cold cocoa and two slices of bread. Fegan's porridge and cocoa wasn't very good when hot, but cold . . . The rest of the meal was spent in silence and all he said was "The next time I blow the whistle I expect you to be quiet". A man of few words was Mr. George, but he meant what he said.

This was not the end of the episode. All those whose numbers he had taken, (yours truly amongst them), were told to report to him on the parade at 10 a.m., where, having checked we were all present, we ran round for another half an hour and were then told to report back at 11 a.m., when the process was repeated, and again at 12 noon and every hour, on the hour, until 4 p.m., when we did our last stint of running that day. Before we were dismissed for the final time, he just quietly said "When I say run, I mean run".

I have always been surprised that some Fegan boy did not win a medal in the Marathon in the Olympic Games, but then, having done so much compulsory running perhaps they decided enough was enough when they left Fegan's.

Lest I give the impression that Mr. George was an unbending disciplinarian and nothing else, I will say there was another side to his personality that he almost tried to hide.

It was almost as if his left hand didn't want his right hand to know what it was doing.

I found out many years later that the Staff of Mr. Fegan's Homes were not, as you might expect from a Charitable Institution, exactly overpaid. Yet very often, on his day off, he would take about three boys to London and give them a very good day out, including meals and a present each. It was also noticeable that he always took the least well-behaved boys and those who never received parcels or visits from other people. It also became apparent that most boys who were lacking a present at Christmas, would receive something from Mr. George. It was always of a very high standard and must have been of considerable cost to himself, when there were so many boys who didn't receive any other help other than that provided by Mr. Fegans Homes.

Most Staff in those days, although reluctant to admit it, had boys whom they liked and favoured more than others, but this could never be levelled at Mr. George. Any boy whom he treated to a day out in London soon found out that the next day there were no special privileges extended to him nor liberties to be taken. And yet this man, who sometimes seemed to be made of steel, had an understanding of the need to show kindness in many other ways that often surprised the recipient.

One day, rather foolishly, I took part in a race across the beds. This was done by running down the dormitory across a row of beds and almost springing from bed to bed. Unfortunately, I slipped and hit my knee against the iron frame of the bed, splitting it open and bruising it quite badly, and, within a few days, it had become very swollen. I reported to the Dispensary, where the Superintendent was in charge, and told him I had fallen over, (but omitted to mention the race across the beds of course). I soon found that I could not straighten my leg and he told me that if I didn't straighten it he would tie a wooden spoon behind it and straighten it that way, and I knew he meant it. Although what good that would have done I do not know. However this remark was overheard by Mr. George, who was assisting in the Dispensary at the time, and the next day when I went for treatment, as soon as I walked in, he said to the Superintendent "I'll deal with his leg" and he did so every day, without using a wooden spoon to straighten it, allowing it to heal up naturally. I was very grateful to him, and not a little surprised, but had he known how the accident occurred it would not have changed his attitude toward me, but when I was fit, I think I would have done a lot of coke-crushing.

Another incident happened about this time. One night, after lights out, a number of us in the top North Wing dormitory were quietly talking in the dark, as we often did (though, of course, talking after lights out was strictly against the rules). Suddenly the lights came on and who should be standing there but Mr. George.

He told us to get out of bed, put our trousers on, and our slippers, as we wore night shirts then (no such thing as pyjamas) and to go down to the parade, where he switched the lights on. There was two or three inches of snow on the ground and he said "Everyone except Sharp start doing press-ups". I was excused because of my knee, but I stood and watched about thirty others doing press-ups in the snow. After a short while he told us to return to the dormitory and get into bed. Then, without any threats about what would happen if we talked again, he switched out the lights and said "Goodnight lads". We all said "Goodnight, Sir" and you could have heard a pin drop. They don't make them like him now.

Mr. George had a great interest in photography, and he possessed a Leika camera and a tripod. Over the years he

Trolleys on the parade, made by the boys using old skate or bed wheels.

took pictures of most of the boys, either in groups or individually, and like everything else he did, he did it really well. Many a Fegan boy has one or two pictures of himself and his friends that wouldn't have been possible without Mr. George and his camera.

I would have loved to have been able to look into his notebook. Whenever he caught a boy climbing across the beams in the bathroom, playing football when he should have been doing some other duty, or the hundred-and-one things that we got up to, out would come his notebook, and that huge grin would spread across his face. He had an uncanny way of appearing at the wrong moment. Sometimes nothing would happen for a few days, but he never forgot and, when some extra task needed doing, out would come his notebook and he would say "Sharp, Smith, Brown and Jones, you seemed to have a lot of spare energy the other day, so you can go and help the gardener for a couple of hours", or whatever it was that needed doing.

One idea of Mr. George that I never quite understood

was that, during school holidays if it was a hot sunny day, then we would have the mid-day meal out on the parade. To do this meant carrying twelve large tables and twenty four long forms out from the Dining Hall and setting them out on the parade, including tables to serve the meal from, plates, knives, forks and spoons, etc. Afterwards they all had to be carried back again, ready to be brought out again the next day. It wasn't as though we didn't spend most of the day in the open air, anyhow. The one disadvantage in this was that, had he have wanted to repeat his running round the parade episode, he would have been limited for room, but I haven't the slightest doubt that, if he had wished to do so, he would have found a way of overcoming the problem, perhaps making us run round the football field.

Mr. George was very fond of running. Perhaps I should rephrase that, he was fond of making us run. I never saw him run once. In fact, he looked the sort of man who would have thought it undignified for him to run. We didn't share his view, as it was part of our everyday life, with fre-

Mr. George – Meals on the Parade in 1945–46.

Mr. Ray Bussell and Junior Boys. Note mat-beater in foreground.

quent cross-country runs, normally to the Aquaduct and back.

One day about twenty five boys ran away at the same time. It caused a lot of excitement as it took the Staff quite a long time to find out exactly who was missing, especially as Fegan boys had developed, to a fine art, the ability of pretending to co-operate, whilst actually doing all they possibly could to hinder, that is, if they thought the occasion warranted it. Why they went nobody was quite sure, but for some reason or other they had had enough of the four walls and led by one or two older boys "took off for the hills". Alas, there were no hills. The surrounding countryside was extremely flat. Some time during the next day, tired, hungry and thirsty, they sat down on the bank at the side of the road at Yardley Gobion, which was about three miles away, when who should appear in his car, yes, the man with the knack of turning up at the wrong moment, – the Deputy Superintendent, Mr. George, himself. He stopped his car, walked over to where they were, and gave one of his famous smiles and said "Well gentlemen, we meet again". He then, in true army fashion, fell them in, in threes, and said "Start running back to Stony Stratford". He, of course, followed in his car.

On the way back a lady Probation Officer, who attended the Chapel, passed them in her car, going in the opposite direction. She was horrified and reported the incident to the Council of Mr. Fegan's Homes, and said that he, Mr. George, "was driving them along the road". She did not realise that if the boys became too tired they would have walked, even if a tank had been following them, and that they would have walked more than they ran, just to be awkward. However, the Council did not take any action, and naturally the usual punishments followed.

So, although we didn't realise it at the time, change was beginning to come, very slowly, and, looking back, I believe the arrival of Mr. George was the beginning.

The routine and the discipline hadn't changed and, although physical punishment and the strap were still in use, they didn't seem to rule our lives as they had done before. The old Superintendent, although still around, had been made General Superintendent of all the three Homes that Fegan's owned – Yardley Gobion (Northants) for the small boys, Stony Stratford (North Bucks) for the majority of school boys, and Goudhurst (Kent) for the boys who had left school at the age of fourteen and who worked on the Farm there until they were seventeen.

So Mr. George held the reins. There was to be no sudden rush into the new era, but here was a man who, although the greatest disciplinarian that I have ever met, was genuinely concerned for the boys in his care, but was convinced, in his heart, that complete change was out of the question as far as Fegan boys went, as it just wouldn't work, for they would take too much of an advantage of anyone who was soft with them.

As for me, I had settled in, and had pushed my days at Enfield and Bounds Green out of my mind as much as I possibly could, although sometimes I was jolted back to reality if I received a letter or when we went for walks and

I saw others who were free to live as I had once done.

Although not exactly happy, I had come to the conclusion that it was all about survival and being tough. Many of the boys confused toughness with roughness, and slowly I was learning that there was more to survival than that.

Somehow or other I had now progressed to being a 1st Squad table boy, not forgetting to put a penny a week in the Bank and also a penny in the collection. This left me with fourpence out of my sixpence pocket money, which made me quite rich by Fegan's standards, although really it made very little difference, as it all had to be spent on sweets. There wasn't anything else to spend it on. I would rather have saved it and gone to watch Spurs or Arsenal play, but I dared not think along those lines for long.

I did have one unexpected setback to my rise in the ranks. One afternoon, when the whistle blew for school parade, a whole bunch of boys ran out of the Bootroom, where they had been cleaning up for school, and although we responded to the whistle straight away, Mr. George didn't think we were fast enough. I was the last boy out, for which he literally gave me a kick up the back-side, and announced to all assembled that Sharp would be demoted to 2nd Squad. I remained there for a few weeks, but, at his suggestion, was put back to 1st Squad. I think he realised that it was rather harsh, considering I hadn't done anything wrong, but, of course, he could not admit that.

Being a 1st Squad table boy also had it's disadvantages, as I was to find out. On all parades there was a roll-call, when the table boys announced who (if any) was missing from their table. If any boys were missing, the table boy would call out to the Housemaster the names, and sometimes the number, of the missing boy. If a boy had the same surname as another boy in the Home, or may be a brother, then he would always be known as, for instance "Smith 45" or whatever his name and number happened to be.

On one such occasion there were so many boys missing that the table boys were told to go and find the absentees. I had three boys missing from my table and, instead of going to look for them, I went into the tiled passage, that went the length of the building, and shouted for them at the top of my voice, and then went into the bathroom to await results. The result was that one of the Housemasters knocked me clean off my feet. Everytime I tried to stand up I was knocked down again. Whoever it was had gone completely berserk. I decided that when I stood up I was going to hit back, but I didn't get the chance as I was knocked round the bathroom like this. Eventually it stopped – probably because the Housemaster in question was exhausted, not to mention how I felt. He then sent me to stand at the platform, but when the others came in for tea he told me to resume my place at the table, That night, when most boys were asleep, the same Housemaster shook me awake, and he had some jam tarts on a plate. I had not seen a jam tart since I had been at Fegan's, but, although I was not bitter about what had happened, I said "No thank you, Sir, I'm not hungry" and went back to sleep. The next day he drew me aside and apologised for what had happened and I accepted this and decided to forget the whole affair.

So things really were changing. It must have been unheard of, up until then, for a boy to get a good hiding and then be offered jam tarts and to get an apology. Come to think of it, it must have been unheard of for a Fegan boy to turn down a plate of jam tarts!

Chapter Seven

Change at Last

The sports field at Fegan's Homes in Stony Stratford was an ideal setting. It was approached by a wide garden path through gardens with immaculate flower borders. The school garden plots were on one side and a large greenhouse on the other. Beyond that were vegetable plots and a walled garden, with fruit trees growing round the walls. (Strictly out of bounds to us, of course). The Stony Stratford Tennis Club was on the other side of the wall.

The sports field itself was hidden from view by two small orchards and could only be seen from the garden path. On one side of the field, and at the far end, was a large meadow belonging to a local farmer, Mr. Toombs, where, in the summer, the cows grazed contentedly. On the other side was the Stony Stratford Sports Ground – also used by the Army during the war years. When not involved in a game of our own, we would watch, through a gap in the hedge, the games of cricket and football played there.

Suddenly one summer evening, when a number of us were engaged in a knock-about game of cricket, one or two of the players stopped playing and ran across to the area of the field where it was possible to look up the garden path. The rest of us soon followed, reasoning that it must be something very important to call a halt to a game of cricket. What we saw was a family of four walking down the path toward the sports field. Someone who seemed to know more than the rest of us, informed us that it was the new Superintendent and his wife with their two children – a boy of about ten or eleven years of age and a daughter who, (although I didn't know it at the time,) was the same age as myself. So at least the "new Man" and his wife knew something about children.

To spare them the embarrassment of being stared at, we quickly carried on with our game and waited, with interest, to see what the change in the heirarchy would bring. The Homes hadn't had a change of Superintendent for about twenty five years, so we were in a rather unique situation, as we awaited the actual changeover to take place.

If anyone had been asked to search the country high and low to find someone who could "change" Mr. Fegan's Homes at Stony Stratford from an Institution to a Home (an impossible task, many thought) then they could not have found two people more suitable than Captain and Mrs. Flood, who were about to embark on a project that, in many ways, their previous life until then had been preparing them for.

Capt. E. P. Flood M.C., M.B.E. had been a peace-time soldier with the Queen's Own Royal West Kent Regiment and was the Regimental Sergeant Major whilst serving in Malta during the second World War. He was then offered a Commission and, having risen to the rank of Captain, was taken prisoner of war by the Germans, following action against the enemy in the Do Decanese on the Island of Leros. He was awarded his Miliary Cross for action during this battle.

One day, whilst a prisoner of war, he was lining up for Apel, (I suppose the equivalent to Fegan's meal and roll-call parades), when one of his fellow Officers complained about the conditions under which they were living.

Capt. Flood pointed out to him that many boys in England lived like that all of the time. The outcome of all this was that he was invited to give a talk to his fellow Officers and prisoners of war on the subject of the needy boys in their own Country. This led to a remarkable decision being taken that, should they survive the war, those present would undertake to open a Boys' Club in England after the war. Varying sums of money were promised to start the work, the amounts being written on scraps of paper available, all promises of which were honoured when the war was over.

Thus was founded the Brunswick Boys Club (so named because the prisoner of war camp that the founders occupied was in Brunswick). The Club is just a short walk away from the Chelsea Football Club. The club was opened by H.R.H. the Duke of Edinburgh and a few years later it became necessary to extend the premises. Having left Fegans Homes by then and donating a modest sum towards the extension, but mainly because of my connections with Capt. Flood, I was invited to the opening of the extension, which again was performed by Prince Philip. Although having a full-time occupation as the Superintendent of Mr. Fegans Homes, Capt. Flood still remained on the Committee of the Brunswick Boys Club in London and often used his one day off a week to perform his duties there.

One day he was asked if he could attend a function at the Club, when he was told that it was intended to show some films of the work there. Having taken his place with the rest of the audience he wasn't at all surprised when Eamonn Andrews appeared with a Big Red Book. Being occupied at nights with Fegan boys, he had never heard of "This is your life" on the Television, until Eamonn Andrews stood in front of him and said the immortal

Lieut. Gen. Sir William Dobbie, G.C.M.G., K.C.B., D.S.O. President of Mr. Fegans Homes inspecting the boys with the Superintendent Capt. E. P. Flood, M.C., M.B.E. (Black boots and Short Trousers).

words, and so, very deservedly, he became a T.V. personality for one night.

Here is a word-for-word repeat of the conversation held by Major Bertie Pond and Eamonn Andrews taken from the script of "This is your life" relating to Capt. Flood (referred to as Major Flood. Although given the rank when prisoner of war he never used the title.).

Major Bertie Pond, formerly of the Queen's Own Royal West Kent Regiment.

Eamonn: When did you two first meet, Major Pond?

Pond: I was in the Queen's Own when Percy joined the Regiment in 1922 or thereabouts. We served in Malta, Palestine, Syria and the Do Decanese. In fact, he took over from me as R.S.M. in Malta when I was commissioned, and three months later he got *his* commission too. Then we were together during the defence of Luqa Aerodrome – that was during the siege of Malta, when he was awarded the M.B.E. for devotion to duty and for the fine example he gave his men.

Eamonn: And where incidentally you received a similar decoration. But that wasn't the only time you met our friend here, when things were pretty hot?

Pond: No. I was on the Island of Leros in the Do Decanese when Flood got his Military Cross.

Eamonn: Do you know the circumstances of his winning the Military Cross?

Pond: He led a very determined attack against the Germans, and, although he got a wound in his leg, he carried on until he gained his objective.

Eamonn: And then again your paths crossed in the prison camp at Brunswick, after a gallant, but unsuccessful, escape attempt in Greece in which you were both fortunate to get away alive. But, Major Pond, you also played a part, many years earlier, in an incident which really has a great bearing on this story we're telling to-night. You know what I mean, I'm sure?

Pond: Yes. What I think you have in mind, Eamonn, happened in Maidstone just about 20 years ago. Percy was a Sgt. Instructor and there was a young fellow who was forever in trouble, always up for some crime or other. I was in charge of the prisoners escort and Flood was there too. The C.O. decided to drop formality and speak to the prisoner man to man. He said "Why do you keep on doing these things?" The boys didn't answer for a while, but at last he said "I'll tell you. You're an Officer. You've had an education. You've got a car and a servant. Look at me – I've been chased by the police, picked up in the gutter, never had any schooling. What chance have I had? I look at you, and I look at me – and I give up".

Eamonn: And it was that incident, I know, that first moved Major Flood to take an interest in the type of person that has been labelled "under-privileged", an incident which flowered in a prisoner of war camp in Germany many years later. Thank you, Major Pond.

A few years later a Fegan boy named Tommy McClean, already mentioned in an earlier Chapter of this book, also became the subject of "This is your life" for his exploits in rowing the Atlantic Ocean single-handed and sailing across it in the smallest boat ever. He was almost the last subject of the programme before the death of Eamonn Andrews.

And so, when Capt. Flood was officially introduced to us as the new Superintendent at the end of the war, not knowing any of his previous history, we just wondered what he would be like and could hardly have dreamed of the changes he was about to implement.

At about the same time as all this was taking place at Stony Stratford a tragic incident happened which was to change the entire field of Child Care, not only in Fegan's but throughout the whole of the Country. It was the death of a young boy who was placed out by a Local Authority with Foster Parents. He died as the result of the brutal treatment dealt to him by his Foster Father, and a Government, which had neglected it's responsibility to the homeless and needy children of this Country, suddenly started to ask questions. A Committee was set up to investigate the problem, and it's Report, entitled "Whose Children?", shocked the Nation. Parliament acted promptly and in 1946 an Act was passed which came to be known as "The Children's Charter", with the Home Office to be the supervisory authority for all aspects of Child Care in Britain.

And so, with changes inevitable, whether particular Homes (however worthy their intentions) liked it or not, there was now a need for leaders and staff to implement the changes. Happily, as far as Fegan's Homes in Stony Stratford was concerned, it was a case of 'Cometh the hour, Cometh the Man'.

As I watched the new man take over little did I then realise the influence he would have on my life and how much sound advice and help I should personally receive from him, especially when I left the Homes and started facing the big outside world.

We got off to a good start when I found out he was a Chelsea supporter just like me, although I had only seen them play once.

Many years later, after he had retired, we used to meet outside Fulham Broadway underground station and then go to watch Chelsea play. When the match was over we used to sit in the stand and let the crowd drift away (very often there was 60,000 people there) while we talked – mainly about Fegan's Homes. It was then that I found out many of the things that happened behind the scenes, of which we boys were quite ignorant.

During such a chat at Chelsea I learned that shortly after he arrived at Fegan's, Mr. George said to him one day "Here, you'll need this" and gave him a rolled up length of strap. On enquiring what it was for he was told it was for punishing the boys, because he would never keep control without it. He took Mr. George to the boiler room and, opening the door of the boiler, threw the strap in. Closing the boiler door he said "If I can't do this job without a strap, I shall not do it at all".

He then went on to explain how he intended to change the Home and to try to soften up the boys and have a good relationship between Staff and boys. Mr. George replied that he didnot believe he would change Fegan Boys but he was prepared to keep the "Scallywags" in order, while Capt. Flood attempted the seemingly impossible.

This did not mean that we now had a soft man at the

helm, who was suddenly going to let everyone do as they liked; rather, we had a very fair and human man who wa going to try to improve our way of life, despite opposition from some who should have known better.

One day at assembly he stood on the Dining Hall platform (where all talks or lectures were given) and he told u that if we wanted to run away it would now be easy, as, during daytime, the large iron front gates would remain open so we could just walk out through the gate instead of climbing over the fence in the field. Also the large metal shutte that was always pulled down in the archway, separating the parade from the front paths and gardens, would also remain open. In fact, I cannot remember it ever being closed again. This may not seem much in itself, but the feeling o being shut in was beginning to go and there was a much more relaxed atmosphere about the place. In fact, it was quite exciting to be there in those early days of change.

Obviously it was going to take time and many of the old tasks and jobs still had to be done, as I was to find out.

It was a Saturday, and by now I was in the Fegan's firs XI at football. In fact, I was still mad about football. On that particular day we played a team from "outside", as we always called it, and we lost. It was not just that we los but that we weren't somehow very sporting about it and grumbled a lot – it was just one of those days. After the match Capt. Flood told us just how badly we had behaved and that some of us senior boys needed taking down a peg or two, and so the eleven of us would have to scrub the Dining Hall floor that night. As I worked on his house and scrubbed floors there, Mrs. Flood had previously told me that I was excused scrubbing in the main building. I then did the worst thing possible and told him this in front o the others, to which he replied in his best Army manner "I've told you to scrub the Dining Hall, and you will scrub it". Oh dear, when would I ever learn? When he had gone I announced to the others that I wasn't going to do it, and so they carried on with it and left my patch, a black strip running down the middle of the Dining Hall like a black carpet. It had now become a big issue, and boys were turning up to have a look and to speculate about the outcome.

s I could not back down and lose face with
nd yet I could not hold out indefinitely.
boy, who was in the Royal Air Force and
few days at Stony Stratford, said to me
) it, you know". I knew he was right, but
it to reply to him, I said "Yes, and I sup-
ny pocket money as well". To my amaze-
ered me a shilling if I scrubbed my patch
: him on, as the other lads accepted that I
a shilling (two week's pocket money) not
ndent, and that made sense to every boy

this event was that, after I had finished
apt. Flood sent for me. He had just fin-
ket money to the others, and he read the
I stood before him with dirty hands and
said "And against my better judgement
you your pocket money" and he gave me
course, didn't know about the shilling,
bed a rich boy. It hadn't been such a bad

nt happened shortly after his arrival, the
did not learn about until one of our visits
lge (Chelsea). It occurred one morning
during the school holidays. In his best
t shouting, but abrupt and to the point –
unced that we were all going down to the
t the grass. Fegan's had a lovely sports
those war years, and shortly after, the
n mown. In fact I well remember Mr.
hbouring farmer) cutting it one year for
urse, meant that we had to keep off it.
g heard this order, the thought ran
d, 'What are we going to cut the grass
nswer was 'dinner knives'. And so over
their way down to the field, armed with a
:ce, where we were split up into groups
cutting the grass. I do not know how the
t my group actually managed to cut a
grass. Although none of us took this exer-

cise very seriously, it was, of course, another diversion from the normal routine and, at the very least, something we had never attempted before. There were a few fights in the various groups and then, after about an hour or so, it was suddenly called off, not by Capt. Flood but by Mrs. Flood (Mum Flood to the boys) because she had so many boys going to the Dispensary with cut hands. So we all went back to doing whatever we had been doing before, and decided that this new chap was slightly mad. In fact, we already thought that anyone who entered Fegan's Homes voluntarily was completely mad anyhow. Then, years later, Capt. Flood told me the full story. It appears that he had gone to the Council of Fegan's Homes to ask for a motor mower, with which to mow the field. The Council told him that they could not afford one. When they heard of the episode of cutting the grass by dinner knives, they said "For goodness sake buy him a mower". The field then became every bit as good, if not better, than the neighbouring Stony Stratford Sports Ground – so good, in fact, that the local schools asked if they could use it for their annual sports competitions, and permission was granted. It also helped to break down any "us and them" complex that had previously existed.

So things were beginning to change. It was not just a well mown sports ground, but the atmosphere of the whole place was changing, and we were beginning to feel part of the real world, rather than being kept isolated from it.

Capt. Flood was often saying that the time was coming when we would be able to go out for walks on our own. Although we didn't doubt that he meant what he said, somehow it just did not seem possible. So, imagine our surprise when he called all the "table boys" together after lunch one Sunday and said "You boys can go out on your own this afternoon, and depending on how you behave will have an effect on how soon all the others will be able to do the same". So off we went and the strange thing was that we didn't know where to go or what to do, and within half an hour most of us were back. But it was a start, and soon it was accepted as a normal thing to do.

When it came round to my Birthday, (apart from being tossed in a blanket until you could touch the ceiling), it was just another day, until, to my amazement, Mrs. Flood came and wished me a happy birthday and then asked me what I would like for a present. I was so surprised that I said the first thing that came into my head, and that was a pen-knife. Off she went up the road to buy me one. After she had gone I realised that it was against the rules to have a knife, but it seemed that even the rules were changing, and I received my pen knife.

Shortly after this I repaid the Floods for their kindness by giving them quite a scare, although it was not done intentionally. One bath night I was sitting in the bath washing myself when the boy in the next bath (which was hidden from me by a six-foot partition) threw a flannel over the top and it landed in my bath. I then threw it back, he returned it until it lodged on top of the partition. I quickly decided that if I climbed up and retrieved it I could look over the top and throw it directly at him, which I did. However, in my haste to get down (completely naked) I slipped and ripped my big toe full length on one of the sharp hooks that the towels hung on. It bled quite badly and soon turned the bath water red. A boy who was still dressed rushed to get Capt. Flood and told him I had cut my toe off. Had you seen the bath water you would have believe that had actually happened. However, they took me to the Dispensary where one of the local Doctors stitched it up and gave me sixpence for being a brave boy. I don't think Capt. Flood was too pleased about this as the whole episode was my fault, but I was certainly doing well financially since his arrival.

The Doctor who stitched me up was Dr. Habgood, who knew something about boys, and his Son became the Archbishop of York.

The Dispensary had played an important role in the daily life of the boys. Now it had ceased to be a place of fear, where boys were sent to be strapped, given castor oil as a punishment and where "runaways" had their hair shaved off. Speaking for myself, however, it was a place I kept well clear of unless I really needed medical attention and could no longer hold out, like the time when I had a septic big toe caused, unknown to me, by an ingrowing toe-nail. For a few weeks I said nothing and hoped it would go away, but one day I was polishing a dormitory floor with a "long arm". (This was a long hinged pole with a fairly heavy block of iron covered with a pad on the end). It was pushed up and down the floor with a piece of blanket beneath it. That day it swung back and hit my toe, after which I could barely walk. So off to the Dispensary I went, and that night was taken across the road to the Doctor's Surgery, where a local Doctor removed the offending toe-nail. At first he took all his "tools" out and I thought he was just going to remove it there and then, but to my relief, he put me under Gas and did it that way. Then it was back to the Sick Bay – a small dormitory reserved for such occasions. My toes were getting used to being bandaged up.

It was whilst in the Sick Bay one afternoon I fell asleep, and when I woke up there was a little girl, about four years old, with her hair in pig-tails, sitting on a chair beside my bed looking at a book. I thought I was dreaming, as there weren't any little girls in Fegan's, but it turned out that a new man was coming to join the Staff, Mr. Mitchell ("Pop" to all the boys) and he was to play a large part in the changes to come. The little girl was his daughter, Heather. Mr. and Mrs. Mitchell lived in a little cottage in Calverton, a village about two miles away. They often invited boys to their home for tea, and any boy who had a Birthday was invited to have tea with them on the following Sunday, and this meant a great deal to us boys.

At first Mrs. Flood took on the task of the Dispensary, but shortly afterwards Fegan's employed a qualified Nurse, Gill Penn, who took a great interest in the boys. Fortunately, she had a tremendous sense of humour, which helped when one day, having my temperature taken, I put the thermometer in the cocoa that had just been brought up, and the poor lady nearly had a fit when she read the temperature. Then I told her what had happened. (The old Superintendent would not have been amused.)

One day at Chelsea, Capt. Flood told me that although a Fegan boy would not hesitate to pull a fast one over the Staff, he would always own up in the end. He then told of how two boys brought another boy into the Dispensary with a terrible gash on his thigh and they told Mrs. Flood that he had cut it on a broken milk bottle, which they produced, at Mrs. Flood's request. Nearly a year later, Capt. Flood, whilst out for a walk with the boys, was passing the old Church Yard, when one of the boys said to him "That's where ... cut his thigh on the railings, when climbing over to get some walnuts". "No", said Capt. Flood, "He did it on a bottle. The boys showed Mrs. Flood the broken bottle". "No, he did it on the railings" said the boy, "We went out and broke a milk bottle to show Mrs. Flood".

I found out later, during one of our chats at the end of a game at Stamford Bridge, that Capt. Flood had two things that he found difficult to cope with during his early days in Fegan's. The first was any waste of food whatsoever. Having known acute hunger as a prisoner-of-war, it angered him if he saw or heard of anyone wasting food or being fussy about what they ate. There should have been no problem with us boys as, although not short of food, we were always hungry and certainly not fussy about it, as nobody was allowed to leave anything on their plate. However, one lunch-time, shortly after his arrival the semolina pudding arrived without any sugar. It appears that the Cook had forgotten to put it in. One or two brave boys pointed this out to Capt. Flood and very angrily he told us that we were lucky to have anything to eat at all, and if we didn't eat it then it would be served again at tea time. Without any vote or discussion, we decided not to eat it. (Fegan boys were very loyal to one another.) And so it came back at Tea-time and the decision had already been made, that we again refuse to eat it. I think there was a feeling that we were made to do so many things against our will, but here was something that they, the Staff, could not make us do. We went hungry to bed and decided to eat it at Breakfast the next morning, although one or two hardy souls again refused and did not eat theirs until lunch-time. And so we felt we had at least put up a fight, and not lost face. It seems that the new man was reaping what the earlier system had sown.

Another thing that happened more than once, which did not make him angry but literally shattered every nerve in his body, was hearing an almighty crash from the direction of the Dining Hall. It was caused by one of the boys, who was washing up, having dropped 30 or more large dinner plates, as he returned them from the scullery to the Dining Hall about 150 yards away. The floor of the passage was quarry tiles, and so the number of broken plates would be quite high. The boys often held a competition to see who could carry the most plates in one go and then somebody would quote an impossible number that had been carried by some boy in 1938 and, unfortunately, there was always one boy who was prepared to have a go- often with disastrous results! What we didn't realise was that in those days, just after the War, it wasn't easy to replace the plates.

However, very much like Mr. George, Capt Flood also had a very human side to him and on a Saturday, only three days before Christmas, he took three boys, myself and two others who were in Fegans' first XI football team, to London to watch Chelsea play against Swansea in the war-time League South, and a wonderful day it turned out to be.

For me this was the first time that I had travelled on the railway since that day in March 1944 when I had first arrived at Stony Stratford, and here I was going back down the same line, but not to Bounds Green but to Stamford Bridge. It was only for a day, but how much it meant to me and the other two boys would have been difficult to put into words.

It was a wonderful day and I well remember, having entered the ground before we took our seats in the stand, Capt. Flood asked one of the Officials if he could take us through the tunnel, used by the players to reach the pitch, and then let us stand on the pitch for a few moments. The Official gave him permission and we felt like royalty, as nobody was allowed on the 'sacred turf' in those days.

Some of the players were still serving in the Armed

A group of Fegan boys at Wolverton Station in 1930s.

Forces, including the man many of the vast crowd had come to see, the England Centre-forward Q.M.S.I. Tommy Lawton. He scored all three goals that day for Chelsea, in a 3–3 draw.

On our way back to Euston Station I invested a penny of my pocket money in a London evening paper that had all the day's football results in it. (No need to wait until Monday when a newspaper was stuck on the notice board in the shed). I was so engrossed in reading it, as I walked along Euston Station, that I fell over a dustbin – and they weren't made of plastic, in those days!

Things were changing when a Fegan boy could openly bring a newspaper back with him after a day out, and share it with his friends; they all had a read of it and I believe it was still doing the rounds two weeks later. It may only seem a small thing now, but it meant a great deal to us boys then.

I was now getting towards the age of fourteen, and so I should be leaving school, and, (after six months or so) leaving Stony Stratford also and going to the Farm at Goudhurst in Kent. So, I was to miss some of the main changes that were to come. Capt. Flood often reminded us that, although we wouldn't benefit from the many things that would soon happen, at least we would be able to say that we were there at the start.

The main change that came about, after I had gone to Goudhurst, was the sending of all the boys to the local schools, which meant that, for the first time Fegan boys would be able to sit the 11+ exams for the Grammer School and 13+ for the Technical College.

"Going out" to school caused a few problems at first, but the advantages were considerable. One boy was given a note, written on a rough piece of paper by one of the Schoolmasters, to give to Capt. Flood and it said "Please take your boys away from our School; we don't want them". In true blunt Army fashion he wrote on the same note "It's your job to teach them, get on with it", and he sent it back to him. About a year later the Writer of the note apologised and said he was happy to teach Fegan boys.

One day, a large group of boys who went to the Wolverton School, arrived back late for tea because somebody threw an apple core at the bus conductor and all of the Fegan boys were made to get off the bus and walk back to Stony Stratford. I'm sure Mr. George must have given one of his famous smiles when he was told of this.

As time passed, many of the boys made friends with other boys in their particular school and often spent a Saturday or Sunday afternoon in their homes, and were made very welcome by the parents. Some lasting friendships were made. The boys also became involved in the other activities of their school and some played football in the morning for their school and again in the afternoon for Fegan's.

To the horror of people who had never had to dig them, the school garden-plots were dug up and raked flat by the boys in their spare time and then turned into a hockey pitch. Capt. Flood was a keen hockey player, having represented the Army and the County of Kent, so he was able to teach the boys the game. Old Boys and visitors, who were now coming in, also enjoyed many a happy game there.

The next move was to have a swimming pool. Previously any swimming had to be done in the local River – the

River Ouse. That was not allowed by the Local Authority during the war, but there was the occasional Housemaster who allowed it during the summer holidays, although we had neither towels nor swimming trunks.

As I have already mentioned, Fegan's Homes was run solely by voluntary donations, and a Council (that hesitated to buy a Motor Mower) was not going to fork out for a swimming pool, but "E.P.F.", as the boys often referred to him, was a very determined man and worked around the problem by dividing the cost of the pool by four and calling the cost of each brick 5/-, and then visitors, friends and supporters of the work, and of course, old Fegan boys, were asked how many bricks they would like to pay for and very soon the money came in. This resulted in not only the boys spending many happy hours on a hot sunny day in the pool, but to most boys, being able to swim extremely well by the time they left. Of course, the local schools asked if they may use it and visitors and old Fegan's boys enjoyed it's benefits too.

I well remember, as an Old Boy, on a very hot summer's evening, having had supper with the Staff, being asked by Capt. Flood to turn the fire alarms on in the North Wing dormitory, while he, and others, turned them on in the rest of the building. After the boys had lined up on the parade and been commended, or otherwise, for their response to the alarm, he then told them they could have a quick dip in the pool before they went back to bed. Things had changed!

Nobody was running away. Where possible, boys were actually going home for holidays and, although there is no substitute for a normal happy family life, everything was being done to make life worthwhile and happy for those who, for varying reasons and for no fault of their own, were deprived of the home-life that many take for granted.

Many more changes were to come. Numbers were reduced by the Home Office. "Working boys", who had left school, became a thing of the past, as the school-leaving age was raised to 15, and later smaller family Homes were introduced. At last, sadly in many ways, the Old

The new swimming pool in the late 1950s.

Orphanage was to close down. Stony Stratford would never be the same again, but all the changes were started by one of the finest men I have ever had the privilege of meeting.

When his time came to retire, a long-standing member of Staff said to him "Although you have maintained discipline and very high standards, I have never heard any Fegan's boy say a bad word about you". That was praise indeed.

Chapter Eight

Camping In Kent

Time was now passing quite happily. I did not feel so trapped or shut in as I had before. I was now fourteen years of age and about to become what Fegan's Homes called "a working boy". This meant that, instead of going to school, I would, with about sixteen other boys, spend the day working around the building doing such work as stoking the boilers, working in the kitchen, gardening, looking after the pigs and poultry and house-boy duties, which included waiting on the Staff at mealtimes, washing up and general domestic work in the Staff quarters. The task I was given was house-boy duties and, although I had done it as a school boy, I hated it as full time work. I almost lived in the Staff quarters and had my meals there in a rather dingy room where the washing up was done, but, of course, my meals were the same as all the other boys. Not the special food the Staff were getting. This was something else that was to change, and the improvement in the meals had to be seen to be believed. But this was to happen after I had left Stony Stratford.

One of the duties as house-boy was to get up early and take the tea round to the Staff and, of course, give them an early call. This was done mainly by knocking on their room door, making sure they answered, and leaving the tea outside. The tea was made in the kitchen and we did have a cup of tea ourselves. Nobody had said we could, but then, on the other hand, nobody had said we couldn't and as there was hardly anybody about at 5.30 in the morning we – the two kitchen boys, the boiler boy and myself – enjoyed the only perk that went with the job.

What I really hated about the house-boy job was that I spent most of every day there on my own and felt cut off from the general life of the place. In fact, I began to feel quite miserable, so I endured it as long as I could and then one day plucked up courage to knock on Capt. Flood's Office door and ask for a change of job. The answer was "No". I had been given a job to do and was to get on with it. A few weeks later I had another try, only to get the same answer, and to be told that if I wasn't careful I would be sent to the Farm in Kent. However, a few weeks later I tried yet again and thought 'I've got to go to the Farm sometime, so here goes,' and shortly after this I was transferred to working in the Dining Hall, Although this was supposed to be a down-grade I felt much happier and did this for my remaining six to seven months at Stony Stratford.

Looking back, it seems that all this was a terrible waste of time as far as the boys were concerned, and what it really did was to get all the work that needed doing about the building done by the boys. There was, of course, no increase in pocket money for what was really full time employment, but even this was to change with the school leaving age rising to 15 and working boys became a thing of the past.

Fegan's Homes had always been keen to take the boys camping, but, unfortunately, the War put a stop to this, for obvious reasons. However, it was decided in the month of August 1946 to take the boys camping to Goudhurst in Kent at a place called Park Farm, which was 2 miles or so from Fegan's own Training Farm, which was rented by them as an addition to their own 346 acres.

This could not have worked out better for me, as I and five other boys, who were due to be transferred to the Farm permanently, were to go with the rest of the boys to the Camp for the whole of August and then straight on to the Farm, without returning to Stony Stratford. Having hardly left the building for $2\frac{1}{2}$ years I was now to get a month's holiday at Camp in the Garden of England.

Capt. Flood, who had spent a lot of time under canvas in his Army days, gave us good advice on how to settle down in our tents for a months duration. All we had between us and the ground was a ground-sheet so we were advised to make a dip in the ground by stamping on the spot with the heel of our boots and so leaving a slight hollow where our hips would be. He also told us to avoid touching the tent from the inside when it was wet as, if we did, the rain would come through. He also suggested the best position to be in the tent (we had seven or eight to a round tent). He gave us one or two other useful tips as well.

So the great day had arrived. The day I once thought would never come, when I was to leave the Home at Stony Stratford for good.

Every boy had two blankets that were rolled up and tied with string, then slung over our necks so that they were carried on our backs. We were to travel by train, then by coach across London. A lot of the strings broke or came undone, but at the end of the day we all managed to still have two blankets each.

It was an exciting day for us. It was only the second time I had been on a train since entering Fegan's Homes and for some boys it was the first time for many years. It couldn't have been an easy task for the Staff to get nearly 200 boys safely to Euston Station, across London by coaches to Victoria and then safely on to Marden Station in the Weald of Kent.

We did not stop for food or drink but that certainly didn't worry any of us as the sun was shining and this was a real adventure for everyone. Some boys had been cooped up at Stony Stratford for the five years of the War, and longer, but here we were sitting in a train travelling through the Garden of England, passing hop fields and orchards with trees laden with fruit, and for once we didn't have to return to Stony Stratford for a whole month, and, in my case, not at all.

The fields that we passed were the fields above which the Battle of Britain had been fought and "the few" (The Royal Air Force) had taken on the might of the German Luftwaffe, having triumphed so splendidly, although at a great cost to many, some of who paid with their lives. At least one old Fegan Boy was amongst them. Then later Kent was to bear the brunt of Hitler's last attempt to defeat this Island, first with the early flying bombs nicknamed "Doodlebugs", many of which were shot down and one actually hit the farm building at Goudhurst with over 60 boys there. Miraculously nobody was badly hurt. Later there were the V2 Rockets that caused such terrible devastation and loss of life.

We, of course, were not mindful of this, as we laughed and joked our way toward what was the first of the "Park Farm" Camps.

At one of the stops the train made on the way to Marden, a gentleman stepped into our carriage and, although we told him politely that he wasn't supposed to enter as our carriages had been reserved, he took no notice, and, as the journey continued, asked us who we were, and where we were going. The boys readily answered his questions and one boy told him that I wasn't going back to Stony Stratford, but would be staying at the Farm. When he alighted, at the Station before ours, he shook hands with me and wished me well for the future. It's strange, but it's something I have never forgotten.

So the train drew into Marden Station and we all alighted. As I looked around me I knew that I was going to like Kent. The corn grew nearly up to the platform and it seemed like a fairyland to me. I will never forget that first day as we arrived at our destination.

The Station was about four miles from the Camp and there were no buses going that way. (I don't think there are any to-day). The lorry from Fegan's Farm was waiting outside and the smallest boys all climbed into the back; the rest started walking. When the lorry had delivered it's first batch of boys it came back for the next load, and the rest of us kept walking, and so on. I was in the last group but did not mind a bit as we walked along country roads with trees hanging over the hedges at the side of the road, laden with plums, apples and pears. I just could not believe how lovely it all was, and, of course, it was very tempting, but the old discipline was there, and we kept walking.

Miss Winifred Pearce wrote in "The Christian" newspaper in 1939 – "Would you see a picture of loveliness that will remain an imperishable memory to the end of life. Then go

Arriving at Marden Station, Kent for Park Farm Camp in 1948.

to Goudhurst on a day in early Spring". I know that this was not early Spring, but August, but it remains an imperishable memory to this day and will do so for the rest of my life. If going to Stony Stratford in those early months of 1944 was a nightmare then going to Kent in 1946 was one of the finest things that has ever happened to me.

When the lorry picked us up and took us the last mile or so, we stopped outside the entrance to the fields were we were going to camp, and we found that all the other boys were sitting by the roadside, waiting to enter. Someone had the idea that we should make a grand entrance, all together, and this we did. There was very little traffic in those days, so there was no problem or risk of anyone being run over while they waited.

We entered Park Farm where two fields had been allotted to us "Stony kids", as the older boys at the Farm called us – forgetting that not so long ago they were "Stony kids" themselves.

The first field had the Dining tent and the cook-house in it. There were also benches for holding a number of aluminium wash bowls, and the toilets were nearby. Also in the first field was an old Oast House that was made use of for storage, first-aid, etc. There was a smallish empty barn, which was also to come in very useful later and a small cow-shed, still in use. The second field had three rows of white tents, already erected. They were round in shape to sleep about seven or eight boys to a tent. So the best position to be was farthest from the entrance, so that nobody had to walk past your bed space to get out.

Once we had been allotted our tents, and the senior boy of each tent had settled any arguments as to where each boy slept, we gratefully put our two blankets down (no pillows) and we all went off for a meal and, of course, more than one cup of tea. The sun still shone, we were in the open-air being looked after by an excellent Staff, and I felt that all that had gone before that day was being put away into the past and I was really happy. Somehow I really felt that I belonged here in this place.

They say that the sun shines on the righteous, that being the case we must have been a very wicked lot, because when we woke the next morning it was raining. In fact, apart from the first day when we arrived, it rained every day for the whole of August, except for three days. That does not mean that it rained the whole of every day, but there were only three days when it did not rain at all.

Author with Rex, Capt. Flood's dog at Park Farm Camp in 1946.

This didn't make life very easy for the boys who worked on the Farm, but this didn't occur to us as we did our best to cope with a very bad summer.

Despite the weather it was a very happy month for all of us, and living out in the open-air we slept soundly, even if we had no beds or special bedding. After sleeping in a dormitory for so long there was something very cosy about a tent, and being only a few of us made it even better. Some nights, when the rain poured down, we had a great sense of security.

Although we all had to lend a hand with the washing-up and one or two other tasks (mainly involved with the Cook-house) there was great freedom about being at the camp, and without abandoning the discipline that we had instilled into us, we had a great deal of fun.

The Training Farm itself was about 2 miles or so away and had it's own swimming pool, which was available to us, and by the time we had walked there and spent an hour or so in the pool and then walked back again, half the day had soon passed. Fegan boys didn't need a great deal of entertaining, so with swimming, cricket, rounders and the odd game of football between the showers time soon sped by. We also had the occasional cross-country run through the woods, which was a novelty to us, and some of the scenery was certainly a thing to remember.

One day it was decided that everyone would walk to Marden Station to watch the Golden Arrow, a famous train of that time, pass through on it's way to London, and most of the boys were very keen to see it. It turned out to be one of the few hot sunny days that we had that month and about mid-morning off they all went, taking sandwiches for lunch with them. I say "they" because I decided to volunteer to help in the Cook-house for the day, and it turned out to be a wise move. The work wasn't too hard and being only a few of us we were treated to cups of tea, cakes and a really special meal at mid-day. About four o'clock the others arrived back from Marden, tired, footsore and very disappointed. When I asked them what the Golden Arrow was like they said "We hardly saw it, as it went through the Station so fast that it was all over in a few seconds". I have never seen the Golden Arrow, but I have no complaints. I thought it was a good day.

I think if I went camping now for a month and it rained most of the time I would feel very unhappy about it, but the strange thing about that "Park Farm" camp was that all the boys enjoyed it. It was a wonderful time for me and I have nothing but happy memories of it.

Whilst it was a great time for the boys, it must have been very difficult for the Staff to know how to occupy us. I well remember one breakfast time, when it rained so hard, that the decision was made to leave us all in the large marquee, as we would have got soaked just going back to our tents.

The Staff went off for breakfast, leaving us unsupervised, which really wasn't very wise. I suppose they thought we couldn't get up to much mischief, just sitting at the tables in the tent. All went well until one boy discovered that one of the Housemasters had left his trilby hat behind, and it was soon being thrown from table to table, and we had a great game with it. Unfortunately, one of the boys, who was in possession of it when the Staff returned, panicked and pushed it into one of the large metal teapots that we used. Strangely, nothing was ever mentioned by any of the Staff. Perhaps they thought it was a small price to pay for keeping 180 or so boys entertained under difficult circumstances.

During the last ten days or so of the camp, the ground around the tents became so muddy that a number of us were transferred to the empty barn next to the cow-shed. Another move that we considered good fun, and we settled down quite well with our ground sheets and two blankets. But we were not to escape being wet completely, as when the Farm boy, who looked after the cows in the adjoining cow-shed, hosed out the cow-shed, some of the water came through the holes in the wall, but this did get rectified when somebody had a word with him. There certainly was an abundance of rain about that year, and the Farm boys were having a difficult time of things, as I was later to find out.

Strip wash at Park Farm Camp in 1948.

Time just seemed to fly by to me and on the last Saturday of the camp six of us were told that we were to go to the Farm and join the other 45 to 50 boys there, all of whom we knew from their Stony Stratford days. So, after lunch, we said our good-byes and left our two blankets behind. My Housemaster gave me half-a-crown, which was a small fortune to me. Capt. Flood shook hands with use and gave us a few words of advice.

One thing he told us, that I have never forgotten, was that we would meet people in the future whose standards were not as high as ours, and that we should not lower our standards to theirs. We would also meet people whose standards were higher than ours and we should try to get our standards up to theirs.

Then we set off, walking on our own to the Farm building, about two miles away, which gave us time to think about the next phase of our lives in Fegan's Homes. We all wondered what awaited us now as we became the only Fegan boys who, on being transferred to the Farm, actually walked there.

Mr. Fegan's Homes Training Farm, Goudhurst, Kent.

Chapter Nine

The Farm

I find it hard to recollect what my thoughts were as we walked along the narrow country roads that led to what was then Mr. Fegan's Homes Training Farm for Boys. For once it wasn't raining, and I certainly felt more optimistic about the future than I did when I first arrived at Stony Stratford.

Being a very remote area, we did not see any other person on our journey, but we did pass a large cottage called Myrtle Cottage, where Mrs, Fegan and her Niece Mrs. Lovell-Keays had been so tragically killed on the 7th October 1943. A German Phosphor bomb landed literally at their feet, probably killing them instantly, and within a short space of time the whole cottage was a mass of flames. A number of the Staff ran to the scene but there was nothing that they could do to help. Attempts were made to get to the room the victims were in, causing injury to Mr. Jack Bramley, one of the Staff. The Cottage had been rebuilt by August 1946 and I never ceased to be amazed that a stray bomb could have hit this building that stood completely on it's own, the nearest dwelling being about a quarter of a mile away.

This was not to be the last time the Boys' Home in Kent would be hit during the War, as later, in 1944, one of Hitler's new weapons, a V.1 flying bomb – a "Doodlebug", was shot down by the R.A.F. and landed alongside the building. It caused considerable damage, but, miraculously nobody was seriously hurt, although the Superintendent received facial injuries and the boys had to evacuate from some of the building and sleep in the Chapel. The R.A.F. Pilot, who shot down the flying bomb, paid a visit to the Farm and told the boys that he was very sorry for the damage that had been inflicted on their home.

The front entrance to the Farm.

However, the War was now over, the building had been repaired and restored to it's original state, and it was almost impossible to see any signs of what had occurred. The only tell-tale result of the bombing was two or three bomb-craters that had been left in the fields and had now filled up with water and looked like quite natural ponds.

And so we arrived at the Farm, which was a very large building, capable of housing about 100 boys, but now housed just over half of that number. It was a two-storey building with a large quadrangle in the centre, often used for a game of quoits.

Although having seen much of the building in the past month, none of us had actually been inside, and were not sure which of the two or three entrances we were supposed to use. Being the Senior boy, I led the others to the front main entrance that, unbeknown to me, was only used by the Members of the Council, Staff and special visitors. Bravely, I knocked on the door, and, after a short pause, one of the Housemasters (the Superintendent was away) opened the door. He was obviously expecting us, and said "Round the back, round the back, don't knock at this door". There was no "Welcome to the Farm lads, I hope you'll be happy here", but we weren't surprised. Stony Stratford had taught us not to expect too much, so we turned away and wondered where the back entrance was, only to be called back and told we might as well go in that way now that we were there but were to use the back entrance in future. The same Housemaster then proceeded to tell us the routine that we would be involved in and which House we would be in. The Houses were named after the places in London where Mr. Fegan opened his first Homes for Needy Boys, Deptford, Greenwhich and Southwark. I was in Greenwich and we were to sleep in the dormitory appointed to each House.

Being Saturday none of us would be required to work until the following Monday, thus giving us a short while to settle in. I found it fairly easy to slip into the routine, as there was so much more freedom than at Stony Stratford.

It was also a luxury to sleep in a real bed again, after sleeping on the ground in the tent, and to wash inside with hot water, after washing outside in cold water, and to be sheltered from the rain, even if we did work out in it.

The water at the Farm was some of the softest water I have ever used. With just ordinary soap you soon had a basin full of bubbles. The water was pumped up from an

Playing Quoits on The Quadrangle at the Farm.

underground well by an electric motor into a tank at the top of a wooden water tower. This was quite a landmark and could be seen from a number of miles away, as the Farm building was at the top of a hill.

Sunday at Goudhurst (the Farm was always referred to as "Goudhurst", although Goudhurst village was over 3 miles away) was a much more relaxed day than at Stony Stratford, even though the cows had to be milked and the horses looked after, the chickens fed and the essential jobs done. Every boy wore long trousers on Sunday and so, at the age of fourteen, I received my first suit with long trousers. The material was the same as the short trousered suit that we had at Stony Stratford. The rest of the week, summer and winter, we wore short trousers on the Farm.

The Farm Chapel was a beautiful building and there was a different preacher every Sunday, many of them coming from London. Some were the same as those that we had heard at Stony Stratford, like Happy Him (Bryant) of the Open Air Mission, who preached at all the big race courses in the country. Another man, who I was to meet many years later whilst on holiday on the Island of Guernsey, was Gipsy Williams.

One Sunday afternoon during that holiday he told me some very interesting things about the real gipsies. Kent had many gipsies in those days and they spent much of their time fruit and hop-picking.

Sometimes, when he came to preach, the old gipsy would ask his daughter to sing to us and she certainly could sing well. You could have heard a pin drop as far as the boys were concerned, and she made a great impression on us all. The Gipsy was really lovely man.

We didn't have a Choir, but the boys used to sing choruses for about 15 minutes before the evening service began, and the sound of those deep voices was really something to be heard. I would give a tremendous amount to walk up the hill one Sunday evening and attend a service in the little Chapel, with the boys singing and dear old Mrs. Stennett playing the organ. I can still hear her playing a piece by Schubert "We would see Jesus", as we

The Farm Chapel.

Interior of the Farm Chapel.

came out of the Chapel at the end of the service. She was the wife of one of the Farm Staff, Bob Stennett, and it would be hard to find two nicer people. No boy ever knocked at Mrs. Stennett's cottage door at Park Farm without being given a glass of lemonade and a piece of cake, and Bob, as we all called him (Sir to his face) often sent a boy to his house, if we were working in the vicinity, to ask his wife the time or some other question, and he always sent a different boy. Years later I realised that he was not really worried about the time, but was being very kind to us boys and would, I believe, have taken all of us home for a cup of tea, but there was no such thing as a tea break allowed on the Farm. I could write a lot about the Stennetts, who also had a Son on the Staff as well, named Reg, and I feel privileged to have met them.

An addition to our wardrobe at the Farm was a sports jacket and a pair of long grey flannel trousers. No-one was allowed into meals with their best suit jacket on. We all changed into the sports jackets.

On Monday morning, as soon as we were called, we went down to the Recreation room and brushed our Sunday suits and had them inspected, so that the boys on the 5 a.m. call for milking, brushed their suit before going out on to the Farm. We were supposed to polish our boots as well, but most of us, unbeknown to the Staff, cleaned them Sunday night. I doubt if there were any other farmers in the country who were brushing suits and having them inspected at 5 a.m. in the morning, before milking cows or cleaning horses etc.

Milking supervised by Mr. Ron Dyer.

The Farm routine was something like this:

5 a.m. First call for boys cleaning cows
5.15 a.m. Call for boys on milking.
5.30 a.m. Call for Horse boys, kitchen boys and boiler boys
6.30 a.m. Call for all the remainder
7 a.m. Breakfast
8 a.m. Parade in the Barnyard for the morning's work
12–1 p.m. Lunch
1 p.m. Parade in the Barnyard for the afternoon's work
5 p.m. Tea
EVENING Recreation e.g. Model making, football, if light.
8.30 p.m. Supper
9 p.m. Bed and lights out.

During harvest, hay-making and fruit-picking time, tea would be taken wherever one happened to be working i.e. the orchard, the hay field, round a hay-stack or in the harvest field etc.

As at Stony Stratford all the cleaning in the Home was done by the boys, including the boilers (but no coke

A house-driven Elevator on the Farm.

Ploughing.

crushing). Two boys helped in the kitchens all day; a boy worked all morning in Blantyre Lodge (once the home of Mr. and Mrs. Fegan but in my time the home of Capt. and Mrs. E. V. Martin, the Secretary of the Homes). Also the Farm Manager and his wife, Mr. and Mrs. Lazell, had a boy working all morning in their house. All this work was done by the new boys from Stony Stratford and after about six months they were replaced, and then worked full-time on the Farm.

My job was cleaning the bathroom. This would have taken all morning at least at Stony Stratford but at Goudhurst I was expected to be out on the Farm by 10.00 hours and Fegan's 10.00 hours was 09.55 hours.

I well remember the first morning asking the duty Housemaster (a man I came to respect and admire – although he did, in his own words, "knock the rough edges off of me" in my early days at the Farm) for inspection of the bathroom, when I had finished it. Without pausing in pace or for breath, as he walked the length of the bathroom, he said "Have you put away the flannels, collected up the soap, cleaned all the basins, polished all the taps, swept under the baths, dusted all the ledges, cleaned all the lamp shades, turned out all the lights?" and, still quoting, disappeared out of the end door into the Bootroom. I knew better than to go and look for him.

And so to work on the Farm. I thought that the first morning and afternoon on the Farm would kill me. We were muck-spreading, which meant that horses and carts would deliver piles of cow manure, at regular intervals, along the field and about twelve or so of us boys would spread it evenly on the ground. I can well remember half way through the afternoon almost praying for a rest and sure enough it was as though my prayers were answered as it started to rain and we had to stand under the trees for about ten minutes. I was hoping it would rain for the rest of the day, but it didn't, and yet somehow that ten minutes made a great difference, and the rest of the afternoon didn't seem so bad. I think that month at camp had made me soft, but I gradually grew stronger as time went on.

Gathering in the Harvest.

The Farm did have it's own swimming pool, and this was a real bonus in the summer when boys would run 'home' (as we called the main building) for a quick swim before lunch. If there was no overtime after tea, quite a long time was spent in the pool, also on Saturday afternoon or evening. All swimming sessions were supervised by a member of the Staff, and, when a whistle was blown, the shortest route to the side of the pool was taken, and we immediately climbed out of the pool. Anyone not doing so risked being banned from swimming for a number of days, according to the judgment of the Duty Master.

The pool didn't have a filter and remained empty during the winter. It was scrubbed clean and washed down at the start of the summer and when the water began to get dirty, and the tiny little red worms began to multiply, then swimming was banned. The pool was emptied by opening a valve by means of turning a small wheel which was let into the ground by the side of the pool. This was never opened fully, as the water had to run away down the hill, through a ditch that eventually passed through a neighbouring farm. Sometimes it took three or four days to empty the pool and then at least another day to clean it.

Once, during a heat wave, the pool had become too dirty to swim in and the Staff reluctantly closed the pool, and opened the valve slightly to allow the water to trickle away slowly. During the night a boy decided to get up, when everybody was fast asleep, and open the valve a little more, to speed up the emptying process. Unknown to him, another boy had also done the same thing and given the wheel a couple more turns. In the morning, when we woke up, the neighbouring farmer's cornfield, at the bottom of the hill, looked like a paddy field, as it was flooded.

The Staff knew, although they couldn't prove it, that the boys were responsible. What they said to the Farmer, I do not know, but there were threats that if it happened again the pool would be closed for a month. We just carried on with cleaning it out as fast as we could so that we could resume swimming again. It also took a long time to fill the pool, but, once it was about a quarter full, we were all very happy.

I can't remember any boy not being able to swim and once a year we held a gala day, when the three houses all competed against each other, and some great times were enjoyed.

I'm sure that being able to swim may well have saved many a boy's life in later years but this, tragically, was not

The Farm Swimming Pool on Gala Day.

to be so in the case of one boy who had left and was working for a Farmer not very many miles away. One hot summer night he went for a swim in the local river, and, although a good swimmer and a very strong lad of about 19 years of age, he was caught in a fast running current and, despite the efforts of another man to save him, he drowned. His funeral was at the Farm Chapel and it cast a shadow over the Farm and amongst many of the boys who had grown up with him.

And so, living in some of the loveliest scenery of the Garden of England, playing football and cricket against teams from the surrounding Villages, and having swimming matches with the nearby Public School (Bethany School), I was happier then than I had ever been in my life. Although working on the Farm was sometimes tough, I really enjoyed it, whether it was in the Dairy, general farming, working with the sheep or driving tractors, which I loved. The only job I wasn't very keen on was fruit farming. Picking fruit was fine, but spraying the trees with Tar-oil Winter Wash stung your hands and face, as we had no protective clothing, and still wore short trousers during the week. Whichever way you went round the trees, the spray blew back on you. There were other

Fruit-picking.

sprays as well. One smelt like bad eggs and so it wasn't a very popular job.

However, after a short while, I was put in charge of the Spray Shed, where the large tanks of spray had to be mixed before it was pumped underground by pipe to the orchards, where, at various points, the hoses were attached, and the boys did the spraying.

The Spray shed, although not very warm, was a lot better than being out in the orchard. The Fruit Master loaned me his pocket watch during the daytime, so that I did not mix up any more spray after 4.30 p.m. So I was official time-keeper as well! Fegan boys didn't have watches, so it was quite a novelty.

Thrashing was a very interesting job, but no place to be if you suffered from Hay Fever (as, a few years later, I found out that I did). I used to tie a scarf over my nose and mouth and although it made me look like Dick Turpin and I received lots of ribbing for it, I found it to be a great help.

Unlike today, when one man on a Combine Harvester cuts and thrashes the wheat all in one process as he drives along the field, in those days the sheaves of corn were collected from the fields having been cut and tied-up by a reaper and binder and stood up in stooks to dry and then stacked to await a convenient day to be thrashed. A lot of corn must have been lost in this process and the rats and mice in the stack lived very well indeed.

The first job before thrashing began, was to erect a small wire fence about a foot high round the stack, so that the rats were delayed long enough for boys with sticks to kill them. The number of dead rats found after two or three days' thrashing was considerable.

The thrashing machine needed an army of boys and staff to work it. Having been lined up and levelled alongside the wheat stack that was to be thrashed, it was driven by a stationary tractor with a revolving pulley on it, and this was connected to the larger pulley on the thrashing machine by a very strong leather belt about 15 to 20 feet long and 6 to 8 inches wide. Boys were not allowed on to the platform to feed the wheat into the machine. This was always done by a member of the Staff. When everyone

Thrashing. Note large driving belt.

was at his post the work began. Usually the work lasted for 4 or 5 days. There was always a boy on chaff and cavings. Cavings were the small pieces of straw which came out underneath the machine onto a large piece of sacking or oil-cloth, and the chaff came out of a chute into a sack. When the sack was nearly full a lever was pushed by hand and the chaff was diverted into a second sack while the first sack was being emptied. As the pile of cavings grew that also had to be removed. Sometimes if the boy on chaff and cavings couldn't keep up with the machine, somebody else might give him a hand, but, if things became really bad, then very often a boy, with the handle of his pitch fork, would push off the leather belt that ran from the tractor to the thrashing machine (after having warned all those nearby). The belt would fly through the air like a wild demon and the boys would shout to the Tractor Master "The belt's off, Sir", which was pretty obvious to him as everything had stopped. By the time he had come down, put the belt back on, lined up the tractor again, the boy on cavings had caught up. Years later, when I met the same Tractor Master he still did not know that it was the boys who pushed the belt off and he said "I always thought that belt came off more than it should have done".

Holidays were not on the curriculum at the Farm, but there were two days in the year when the boys went to Maidstone for the day. Once, I believe, in the Spring and again in late Autumn. The Farm, of course, had to be kept running, so we were divided into two groups. Half the boys remained behind while the first group went, and then the following week those who had not been took their turn. If you happened to be on milking or horses then you still did those duties before going off to Maidstone after breakfast, in the Farm lorry. I understand that prior to this the boys walked to Maidstone. It was about 13 miles, so we were the lucky ones. We were given a small amount of spending money and I can still hear the Superintendent telling us that "A fool and his money soon part company". Having alighted in a car park, near the market place in Maidstone, we usually spent the morning looking around the market and the shops. In the afternoon everyone went to the pictures. One year, another boy and myself, each decided to buy a rabbit. We had prepared a couple of hutches and had permission to put them at the edge of a

Arriving at Maidstone in the Farm Lorry in 1948.

Work parade at the Farm.

sheltered spot, not far from the swimming pool. We watched the rabbits being auctioned in the market, but did not dare join in, and one of the stall holders asked us what we wanted. When we told him, he sold us two rabbits for 2/6d. each. One was all black and one was a chinchilla. I owned the black one. We put them in a cardboard box and then remembered that we wanted to go to the Pictures, and so decided to take them with us. They survived the ordeal extremely well, and a few weeks later my one had a family. This was the start of a very flourishing pet club. For some reason, the Farm Manager didn't approve, but could not intervene. Perhaps he didn't like us using the Farm's hay and the occasional bit of kale etc. Why, I don't know, as the small amount we needed hardly made any difference to the fields of kale and numerous hay-stacks that there were on the Farm. The rabbits really thrived and were well looked after. The only sad part about this was that I had to leave mine behind when I left, so I gave them to another boy, and often wondered how they survived.

Once, instead of going to Maidstone, we spent a day at Hastings, which was only about 20 miles away, travelling by Coach. This was a far better day out, and we all went together. The Farm Staff did the milking etc. to the great delight of the boys.

It's hard to put into words how much I loved the Farm, although it was hard work and sometimes long hours. I spent six months of 5 o'clock milking without one day's break and it was hard not to fall asleep during that period at services, in the Chapel. One boy did fall fast asleep when the General Secretary of the Homes was preaching, and suddenly he spotted him and stopped preaching saying "Wake that boy up, I have something important to tell him".

Looking back, I believe I was at Goudhurst in what must have been it's best years for the boys. The War was over and there was a great atmosphere all round, and it wasn't until I had left that I realised how happy I had been.

The Staff, both on the Farm and in the Home, were really outstanding people and treated us very well indeed. In fact, I can only ever remember one boy being hit by a member of Staff and it led to quite an unusual incident.

It happened at breakfast time one morning. A boy accidentally knocked over a jug of cocoa and the deputy Superintendent struck the boy whom he thought had done it. But he had picked the wrong boy. The boy in question punched the deputy Superintendent straight between the eyes, knocking his glasses flying. He then picked up his two slices of bread and ran, disappearing out of the Dining Hall, leaving the door swinging behind him and we did not see him again for at least two weeks.

In the $2\frac{1}{2}$ years that I was at Goudhurst, this was the only time that a boy had ever run away and nobody seemed to know where he had gone. I personally assumed that he was living in the nearby woods and one or two of the boys were smuggling food out to him. It was early winter, and the Staff, although not admitting it, were beginning to get worried. Then, one evening after about a fortnight, one of the Housemasters went into one of the modelling rooms, where the boys were making model galleons, and who should be sitting there but our missing boy. "So you have come back then?" said the Housemaster. "Yes, Sir" replied the boy, and off to the Superintendent they went. The Superintendent refused to take any action, as he said not only had the boy been provoked, but also the Deputy had wrongly picked on him. That it seems was the end of the matter, until one Saturday the boy in question asked me if I would give him a hand, and he took me up a ladder that led into the loft, and there he had a mattress and a pile of books. He told me that when he ran out of the Dining Hall, after punching the Deputy Superintendent, he ran straight up the stairs and up the ladder into the loft. Then, when the boys were out on the Farm, he managed to carry a mattress up to the loft, and lived there for two weeks, coming down and collecting some food when the boys had gone out to work on the Farm. In the evening, he would come down and spend the time in the Modelling room, with the door locked, amongst about four other boys who were making their models, until the night when the Housemaster insisted that they open the door and it was assumed that the runaway had returned. I helped him down with the mattress and the books and to this day, as far as I know, the Staff do not know that the boy they thought was out sleeping rough was fast asleep in the loft with access to a daily supply of food.

One period that I have not mentioned during my time at Goudhurst was when I was given the job of Post-boy. For some reason that nobody quite understood, the Postman did not deliver the post to the Farm or to the Farm Staff, so a boy was given the job. I was asked to do it during the 1947 Winter, when it snowed for months and was one of the worst winters on record in this country.

Every morning, at 6.30 a.m., I took the farm bicycle out of the small room near the side entrance to the Farm, where it was kept. It had a small front wheel and a carrier just above it, like the old grocery delivery bikes used to be. Dressed in short trousers, socks, shoes, pullover and a jacket, over which I had an old war-time Gas Cape (overcoats and gloves were unheard of), I cycled the three miles to Goudhurst Village to collect the post and the daily newspapers. I was given a leather satchel, with a lock on it. The outgoing post from Fegan's was put in the satchel which was locked by a member of the Staff. When I arrived at Goudhurst Village a Postman (who to my annoyance often called me "Sonny") unlocked the satchel, took out the outgoing post and put in the post for the Homes and Staff and then locked the satchel. So far so good. I then cycled down the hill to the paper shop, close to the pond in the centre of Goudhurst Village. The paper shop was seldom open when I arrived there and I normally had to stand outside in the snow while the shopkeeper went another mile or so down the hill to Goudhurst Railway Station to collect the papers. So sometime between 7 and 8 a.m. I put the papers into the bicycle's carrier and returned to the Farm, delivering the papers to the Farm Staff on the way (still not having had a cup of tea or breakfast). If I was very late I had to explain that the paper shop was not open and I had to wait.

Having done all this, and handed in the locked satchel to one of the Staff, I put the bicycle safely away and made my last delivery, before a late coldish breakfast. This was the News Chronicle to the Cook, a well-meaning lady, but rather abrupt. Most mornings I would walk into the kitchen, still freezing cold, and say "Here's your paper Mum" and she would reply "Put it in the drawer boy. I haven't time to read it". However, when she eventually left Fegan's, after over twenty years' service, she did thank me for pumping up the tyres of her bicycle every week.

In the evening at 5 p.m. I repeated the journey, but only for the post. One night, in the snow, the bicycle slipped from under me as I was going down the hill from the Farm and I slid across the road into the path of the Farm Tilly or Jeep. When I looked up I was looking at the tyres, it had stopped inches away from me. I gratefully got up, brushed the snow off myself, picked up the undamaged bicycle and cycled off to Goudhurst Village – the post had to be delivered.

After doing this job for sixth months, whilst waiting for the paper man to open up his shop, the top window of his building blew open and the broken glass fell on me, most of it hitting me on my back. When I reported this to Capt. Martin, after again having been asked why I was so late returning, he decided that enough was enough and within a fortnight a new paper man had been found who would deliver the papers himself to the Farm. He also asked the Post Office officials to deliver the post – and so I became redundant.

The post job also meant that you became the Office boy during the day and general factotum. During this time I was offered the opportunity to leave the Farm and become the Office boy in Fegan's Head Office in London, which would have meant leaving the Farm at least a year earlier than I did. I turned down this chance and another boy went in my place. Everybody thought I was mad, but it was the best decision I have ever made, as by now I loved Goudhurst and there is a part of me that is still there. So I quite happily returned to working on the Farm.

Whilst reminiscing about cooks, my mind turns to food at Goudhurst which was very similar to that at Stony Stratford and the menu remained the same for every week of the year, except, of course, Christmas. However, a new Superintendent arrived after I had been there for about a year and he announced that the Staff and boys would have the same food to eat. So this meant that either the boys would have the same food as the Staff or the Staff would have the same food as the boys. The outcome was that the boys would now have the same food as the Staff and very nice it was too. Even Goudhurst was learning to change!

Considering that there were nearly 50 boys on the Farm, with a considerable amount of machinery, tractors, a thrashing machine, one or two grinding and rolling machines in the granary, 5 Shire Horses, a massive bull and a large herd of cows, there were very few accidents. The most serious was when a boy stood in front of the mower blades of a tractor and, as he was cleaning the blades, the clutch-clip on the tractor slipped and the blades went into his foot. But for the quick reaction of the Tractor Master the boy would have lost his foot. Although he spent some time in hospital, his leg eventually made a complete recovery. Some put this down to the fact that every morning, for five or ten minutes before the boys paraded for work, the members of the Farm Staff all met in the Stables – with the Shire Horses there (Prince, Captain, Boxer, Punch and Champion) and prayed for the boys and the work of the day. Later on, when I was in the R.A.F. and visiting, I was privileged to attend this prayer meeting and it is something I will never forget.

I do not know how Fegan's Homes chose it's Staff, but, however it was done, they had some really exceptional people.

I did meet one ex-member of the Staff, who applied for a post as Housemaster when Mr. Fegan was alive, and he told me that Mr. Fegan invited him to the Farm for the weekend, so that they could have a look at him and he could have a look at them. The gentleman in question lived in Brighton so he travelled by train to Marden Station and cycled the rest of the journey, having brought his bicycle with him, in the goods van of the train. On the Monday, when he left to go back to Brighton, Mr. Fegan gave him an early call and a cup of tea, and off he went in the dark toward Marden Station. A few months later, when he had been working for Fegan's for a week or two, Mr. Fegan reminded him of that Monday morning, and asked him how he had managed. He told Mr. Fegan that he had hardly reached the bottom of the first hill when the oil in his front lamp ran out and he couldn't then see the sign posts. Not knowing the way, he had to strike a match at every one he came to. Also his saddle became loose, making it difficult to ride the bike, and he only just caught the train. He then said "You know, I think the boys let the oil out of my lamp and loosened my saddle". Mr. Fegan replied "No, they didn't, I did, and if you hadn't caught the train, you wouldn't have been given the job."

In the same way that changes had come about at Stony Stratford, and were still happening, so small changes were filtering in at Goudhurst. The routine on the Farm and the pocket money didn't alter though, and here is an interesting list of it at the end of 1925, which was almost the same as in 1946.

Seniors   2/6d.   1st Squad 1/-   3rd Squad 6d.
                           2nd Squad 8d.   4th Squad 4d.

Defaulters stood up for meals, went without their second course and would be given extra work.

The Defaulters had, thank goodness, been abolished by 1946, although there was a marking system for work on the Farm. Every boy was given marks out of ten for a morning's work and an afternoon, also for Saturday morning. If a boy received ten marks, he was paid an extra penny with his pocket money, giving a boy 11d. a week extra. This rarely happened. The marks went down in twos and so an average mark was 8, and if a boy received a low mark i.e. 4 or 2, questions were asked in the Home, and it could affect his Squad. If a boy did something bad on the Farm, he could be given no marks at all '0'. This meant he lost all of his pocket money. So, if a boy did something wrong on Monday morning, and received a 'Duck' (as it was called – '0') no matter how hard he worked for the rest of the week, he wasn't going to be paid on Saturday. I always felt it was a very bad rule. Once, another boy and I were given the job of repairing the swimming pool shed roof, while the Master in charge of us was on holiday for a fortnight. When the Secretary of the Homes found that we hadn't any marks, he said that he would mark us, and he gave us both tens for every day, including Saturday mornings, for the whole two weeks. It was probably the only time this had ever happened in the history of the Farm!

One of the changes that was very much appreciated by the boys was when one of the Housemasters decided to get up, even earlier than usual, and make jugs of cocoa, so that every boy had a hot drink before starting the milking and cleaning the horses etc. at 5 a.m. onwards. This later was extended to all boys and it was great to get up in the morning and start the day with a cup of very well-made cocoa.

Another change that made a big difference to us was the new "Sunday suits" that were then being issued. They matched anything that was being worn by the boys in the nearby "Public School", in a lovely array of blues, browns and greys. I had a grey one and I would be proud to wear it now. It was a great improvement on the old drab Fegan's worsted that we had worn for years and made us all look the same.

But one thing didn't change, and I believe rightly so – the old discipline, not even with the new Superintendent. One Saturday afternoon a group of about six of us boys were invited to Goudhurst to a party. This really was something. It was at the house of Miss Humphries who was in charge of the Office at the Farm, and, of course, had been in charge of me when I was the Office boy. It was a lovely sunny day and we walked to Goudhurst, having been warned by the new Superintendent to be on our best behaviour. Shortly after our arrival we had tea and we just could not believe the amount and variety of food that was on the table. Miss Humphries and her guests made a great fuss of us and kept offering us more cake, pie, trifle. You name it, it was there, and lemonade galore. We had to leave before the party was over, as we were not allowed to remain out late and I can remember to this day how we walked back to the Farm. We laughed and joked every inch of the three miles, we were so happy. In fact, we felt we could do anything, and that was our undoing. Once more, instead of going into the building by the usual back entrance I boldly led them to the side door, where the "post" bicycle was kept, and, finding it locked, I stupidly banged on the small window of the door, with my fist, and sure enough it went through the glass and cut my hand quite badly. The Superintendent hearing the noise came and opened the door. He looked at my hand, then he looked at the broken window, and said "You'll have to pay for it Sharp". We were back! And so the best two and a half years of my life were beginning to draw to their close. I had been made Captain of my house, Greenwich, which in the past had won very little, and now, in my final year, we managed to win every cup that we competed for, Football, Cricket, Swimming, Athletics and, believe it or not, the Conduct award.

For the first time in my life I felt that I really belonged, and now, at the age of seventeen, like all the boys at Goudhurst I was to be found a job on a farm and a place to

The Recreation Room at the Farm.

live with people that I did not know, and I was to find that leaving Fegan's was as hard, if not harder, than first going to Stony Stratford.

Some boys took to their new farms and surroundings quite well. Others found it difficult after being surrounded by so many boys and Staff. To then find themselves living with complete strangers, in a small house, was too much. It took me years to get used to living in a house, after the large buildings of Stony Stratford and Goudhurst.

My last day on the Farm was a very sad day indeed and I did not realise how difficult life was going to be in the next year or so. I drove the tractor, a Fordson Major, for the last time and put it away in the shed that was only just wide enough for it. Most nights I would have locked the door and left it quite happily, but that night I wanted it absolutely right and so I drove it out again and, in my efforts to get it perfect, I bumped into the garage where the Farm lorry was kept. The garage was made of wood and the starter handle of the tractor put a small hole in the side of the Garage. I decided to say nothing. Later Mr. Bramley, who drove the lorry, sent for me and before he spoke I said "I know why you want to see me" and I told him about the hole in garage. He didn't know anything about the hole. He just wanted to invite me to his house to tea.

I wish to draw a blind over that first year after I left Goudhurst. I then did my National Service in the R.A.F., which I loved, and it gave me a chance to get used to the world, that I had been shut away from for five years, and I found difficult to cope with after those very happy days on the Farm.

Alas, it was decided to close the Farm in 1953 and open a smaller one at Buxted in Sussex, as the boys at Stony Stratford were now sitting the 11+ exam and many were going to the Grammar and Technical Schools. Also the school-leaving age had been raised from 14 to 15 and, of course, not every boy wanted to be a Farmer.

The Farm at Goudhurst is now a Prison, called "Blantyre House", and does very good work in helping prisoners toward rehabilitation. The Prison Officials kindly invited about 50 old Fegan boys back to have a look round the building, and most of us felt that the Prisoners had an easier life than we did. I would not have changed the days I spent there. I still go back to have a look around and remember the past.

If it was possible I would happily turn the clock back and spend my two-and-a-half years there again, but this time they would have great difficulty in getting me to leave.

Chapter Ten

Old boys and reunions

The moment I put my case into the boot of the car that was to take me to Marden Station and I took my last look back at the building at the top of the hill which had been my home for $2\frac{1}{2}$ years, I became an Old Fegan Boy. Although I would rather have remained at Goudhurst, I was and still am, proud to be an Old Fegan Boy.

Looking back, I feel that leaving your familar surroundings and all your friends and to suddenly find yourself living in a tiny house with people you have never seen before, is a great shock. Some boys were very fortunate in that they worked and lived with people that they took to straight away, but this was usually an exception to the rule. I remember my first Saturday after I had left, thinking "They are all playing football at Goudhurst now". I would have loved to have been back there with them.

Starting a new job isn't always easy, but most children doing this go back to their own homes at night, and, however much they may dislike their work, at least they can talk it over with their family and friends, but a Fegan boy had nobody to share his feelings with. He was just expected to grin and bear it.

Not many boys stayed in their first job, although most had to stay for a while as they had very little money and no where to go. Boys were never taken to see their new place of work or where they would live, and given the chance to say "I would rather try somewhere else".

There are some very sad stories about how some were treated when they arrived, and, although they had the best of treatment at Goudhurst, nobody was given any advice or help about leaving. It was rather like teaching someone to swim and then throwing them in the deep end of the pool, and walking away and leaving them.

One boy told me that the Superintendent of his day took him to Marden Station, gave him his case and railway ticket and said "Well Smithers (that wasn't his name) work or starve" and drove away and left him. That boy had been in Fegan's Homes since he was four and had never travelled on a train on his own before, and had to find his way across London on the Underground to get the connection for his next train. Fortunately, he was going to a good job and lived with some very kind people and remained with them for the rest of his working life.

One boy who left went to work for a member of the Council of the Homes and he wondered what book he could leave beside the boy's bed for him to read (reading in bed wasn't allowed in Fegan's in those days). He decided against a Bible and opted for a book on Cricket by Dennis Compton, which was evidently the right choice, as he said the light was on until after midnight in the boy's room. Not all boys were so fortunate as this.

On leaving, each boy was given a new Suit and I have since managed to obtain a copy of the list of clothes that I received when I left. We were also given a new Case (I still have mine) and any money that we had in the Bank. I believe I had 10/- (50p.)

```
        BOY'S OUTFIT              No. 5449
Name:   S. Sharp                  Date: 14.2.49.
        1  Case                   4  Handkerchiefs.
                                  1  Hair brush
                                  1  Clothes brush
        1  Suit                   1  Tooth brush
        1  Raincoat               1  Comb
        1  pr. Working Trousers   Studs
        1  Working Jacket         Laces
        2  Suits Overalls         2  Prs. Pants
        1  pr. Working Boots      2  Vests
        1  pr. Wellingtons
        1  pr. Sunday Shoes       1  Pullover
        1  pr. Slippers
        2  Working Shirts         BIBLE
        1  Radiac Shirt           DAILY LIGHT
        2  Collars
        2  Suits Pyjamas
        3  prs. Socks
        1  Belt
        1  Tie                    Signed S. Sharp
```

At one time, every boy in Fegan's had to go to the Farm, unless of course any relations he had (not every boy was an orphan) asked for him to return home. Not many boys remained as farmers, and, like boys the world over, they soon began to turn their hand to a variety of ways to earn a living.

Quite a number joined the Armed Forces, as they were used to the communal life that it offered, together with the opportunity of taking part in a variety of sporting activities. The discipline, of course, came easy to them. Most of them really wanted a home of their own, and the majority of boys eventually settled down very well and have made a good life for themselves.

Fegan's Homes did it's best to keep in touch with the Old Boys (and still does to-day) through a magazine that came out quarterly, called the "Home Link" and, of course, boys were always welcome to visit the Old Homes. Some actually stayed for a week or so and some visited for just a day or a weekend. When the Farm at Goudhurst was sold this left only the Home at Stony Stratford to visit, and, as time went on, the Staff that were there in your time had left and the new Staff did not know you.

However, one old Fegan's boy, who was in the Army during the War, was visiting Stony Stratford, and one night during an Air Raid said to the Superintendent "Why can't we have Old Boys' Re-unions like they do at Public Schools?" And so the idea took root. As soon as the War had ended in 1945 the first Old Boys' Re-union was held at Stony Stratford for a whole weekend, and being the Whitsun Bank Holiday it lasted for Saturday, Sunday and Monday, with some boys arriving on Friday night.

This first Old Boys' Re-union was attended by about 50 boys. The numbers remained fairly consistent at all Re-unions, which were then held annually at Stony Stratford with the exception of the second one which was held at Goudhurst. I was still a boy in the Home when the first Re-union was held, but we found it very exciting and I enjoyed listening to all the stories that

An old Fegan Boys' Football Team. The Author is standing 2nd from left.

were being told and, of course, it was much tougher in those days than in ours! In some way that may have been true and, if it was, I am glad I had not been around to witness it.

The Old Boys played the present boys football and cricket, and they hadn't forgotten how to play. Although the result didn't matter, they won quite easily and it did us good to find out that we were not invincible. Later on Hockey was added to the games that we played together.

Another tradition that Fegans held was called "Penny on the Wicket". There were a number of trees around the edges of the playground at Stony Stratford and two of them, one at each end of the playground, were called the "bowling-up trees". Generations of Fegan boys had made a mark horizontally across these trees at the same height, as a set of cricket stumps, and, with the aid of two old cricket bats, any boy with a tennis ball would bowl to the boy batting. Whoever bowled him out would take his place and he would then bowl with the ball of the boy who had got him out. Catches didn't count.

Sometimes ten or more boys would be lining up to bowl. When the game was over, usually because of school parade or meals, each boy would have his own tennis ball back (mainly provided by the kindness of Stony Stratford Tennis Club) and one boy would hide the bat until the next opportunity to play. When the Old Boys arrived, one of them would bat and when a boy bowled him out he would throw the boy a penny and carry on batting until he ran out of pennies. Then another Old Boy would take his place. There was only one rule. Nobody was allowed to "poke" i.e. play a straight bat. Some of the Old Boys hadn't forgotten how to hit a ball, but the present boys did quite well out of it and the Old Boys would sometimes deliberately miss a ball to the not-so-good bowlers. It was hard to believe then that one day I would be batting and handing out the pennies.

Anyone missing these Reunions really did miss something. The Old Boys usually slept in a Dormitory on mattresses on the floor, but it didn't matter as sleep was not the priority. Half the night was spent talking about old times.

I have always found that whenever I have met an Old Fegan Boy it didn't matter if I had not seen him before or if he was of a different generation to me; within a short time it was as though I had known him all my life. The same applied to the boys who had gone to Canada, when they left the Homes and came back to visit.

In fact, I have always felt that there was something special about the Canadian boys. Some have referred to it as "the Fegan Spirit" and I have certainly never found it anywhere else.

The second Reunion was at Goudhurst and again I was still a Fegan boy for this, but I can remember it well. The weather was perfect and, as well as the usual football and cricket matches, we held a sports day. There was, of course, no "Penny-on-the-wicket" at Goudhurst, but I do remember one Old Boy asking me if I would mind polishing his shoes, which I willingly did, and, to my amazement, he gave me 2/6d, which was more than I earned in a week on the Farm. When I attended the Re-unions myself as an Old Boy, I became very friendly with this particular boy and found out that he had been in the same Regiment as Capt. Flood and had also been a Prisoner of War. His name was Herbert Sharp (but no relation of mine though).

And so the Re-unions went on and became an Annual event at Stony Stratford, as the Farm at Goudhurst was now closed. Much of the success of these Re-unions must be attributed to Capt. Flood, who, with his Staff, took on a lot of extra work for three days, as well as looking after the present boys. All the Old Boys had a great respect for Capt. Flood and this included the ones who hadnot been in the Homes under his leadership. I think these Re-unions were unique and I doubt if any other school or organisation had anything to compare with them. It always took a few days to get over them, mainly because we were all tired out, but also there was a great sadness when all our friends, who meant so much to us, would then be scattered about the Country and we would not be seeing them for at least another year.

So what did the boys do when they left Fegan's? For many years after leaving the Farm they all went to Canada, but, of course, the Second World War put an end to all of this, and, for reasons I have already explained, it was not resumed again after the War. Although I am reluctant to single out boys who were successful, as it is very difficult to assess "success". there are, however, some interesting stories of what happened to various boys, after they left Fegan's Homes, that are worth recording.

One boy whom I met on a number of occasions, but was in Fegan's Homes before my time, owned a fleet of buses in Toronto. One day I asked him how he did it on twopence a week pocket money, and he told me that when he went to Canada with a group of other boys, he was sent to work on a Farm and did not really like it and so, after a while, he took a job working in the local Store. Local Stores in Canada, in those days, had the monopoly of most of the trade, but he then made his master move and married the Store – keeper's daughter. He had a family, who have now grown up and one Son carries on the business. So, having received some help at the beginning, he still worked hard and took risks to run a successful business, and was a really pleasant person to meet and a very respected citizen of Toronto.

Another boy who left the Farm at Buxted went to work for a Landscape Gardener, who, after a year or two, retired. The boy bought the business, which was a few lawnmowers and a couple of rollers. Then the 1963 Winter set in with weeks of snow and frost and, of course, he had no work to do. During this time he was offered the chance to buy some "Tar Macadam" equipment and, against much advice not to, borrowed some money and took a risk. When the Winter was over he spent the next two or three years repairing driveways that had been broken up by the severe weather. He now runs a large business laying new surfaces on roads, airports and other such large contracts.

Another boy in the South of England, from small beginnings, built a number of blocks of flats on the South Coast, including some near the beach at Bognor Regis.

Arthur—, when he left the Homes, found his way into the Film industry and those who knew him at Stony Stratford were not surprised one day to see his picture in a London evening paper escorting Princess Margaret around a Film Studio. As a boy he was an outstanding Cricketer and many seriously believed that, had he taken up the game professionally, he may well have represented his Country.

Many Fegan boys were, of course, involved in the two World Wars. Unfortunately there is no record of those who laid down their lives for the freedom of others. One that we did hear about, when I was a boy at Stony Stratford and had paid a visit to us whilst training as an Officer in the Air Crew of the R.A.F., was Ernest Kelly, who failed to return from a bombing raid over Germany. No news was ever given of what happened on that fatal night.

Amongst the boys who came over from Canada to a recent Reunion was one who is a retired Headmaster and two who were fully qualified Church Ministers.

It would be wrong to conclude this Chapter without mentioning Tony Spencer, who was a boy at Stony Stratford when I was there. Having served some years in the Royal Navy, Tony then worked as a technical representative for a firm and had the misfortune to lose the use of his right arm, due to illness, and so had to give up his work. Prior to that he had not been an artist, having never painted before, but he taught himself to paint pictures, using his left hand. He now regularly holds an Exhibition of his paintings in an Art Gallery in Portsmouth and many of his works have been sold. He recently painted a picture of the Boy's Home at Stony Stratford, complete with the Steeple, copied from a photo taken in the 1930s. Prints of this picture now hang in many Old Fegan Boys' houses in various parts of this Country, Canada and even Northern Ireland, and it is an excellent painting.

It may be of interest to mention that a year after leaving Goudhurst I entered the R.A.F. for two years' National Service. On leaving I joined the Civil Service.

Having completed 38 years with the Civil Service I am now retired and can devote more time to my garden (and writing a Book about Fegan's Homes).

And so the list is endless and we could mention many others, including the greater majority who, despite many

Photograph of the Picture painted by Tony Spencer of the Boy's Home at Stony Stratford.

set-backs and difficulties in their early life, have become respected citizens in many parts of the world and are a credit to the work of Mr. Fegan's Homes for Boys, and later on, of course, for girls.

Chapter Eleven

Canada

In 1884, at the suggestion of Lord Blantyre, Mr. Fegan took ten boys to Canada and was so pleased with what he saw of that Country that he sent another 50 boys that Summer.

Fegan Boys in Canada, just landed and waiting for the Toronto Train – about 1912–13.

Little is known about those days and so one must use one's imagination and try to get into the mind of one of the boys arriving in a new Country from England.

Many of the pictures that have been found in the present day Head Office of the Homes show that some of the boys who went were very young, thus the ages and physical size of the boys varied considerably and, although it was a different age to the present one we live in, I personally have always felt for the younger boys who not only found themselves in a strange Country but often on Farms literally miles from any town, and at the mercy of people whose main interest was the amount of work that they could do. Although some were fortunate in the "folk" who employed them and gave them shelter, others were not so, and having lived with so many other boys for a number of years and then suddenly to find oneself alone on a vast farm in Canada, must have been a shattering experience.

One such boy was John M Martin, whose parents had died by the time he was eleven years of age and he was placed in the Orphanage at Stony Stratford at the age of twelve. He was sent to Canada, with 59 other boys, and was hired out to ranches and lumber camps for $24 a year, and for the next five years had no schooling. At the age of seventeen he went to the United States, determined to improve his lot. Working his way through Doane Academy, he went on to earn his B.A. at Denison University in Ohio and later his M.A. in the field of Speech at Wittenberg University. World War I interrupted his education. He served as an Officer with the A.E.F. in France and there earned his U.S. Citizenship. He then taught Speech and Dramatics for 21 years. In 1953 his pupils at the Oakwood High School, Dayton, won the national championship at the Forensic League Finals in Denver. That same year Denison University cited him for outstanding work in his field. John Martin has not confined himself to teaching and is the author of at least three books, including a book of poems entitled "Things that make the Home endure", of which I am fortunate to have a copy. He is also the Father of four daughters, his only Son having lost his life in World War II.

Many other boys who went to Canada made a new life for themselves and many, it seems, we know very little about. As has been previously mentioned, in 1910 Mr. Fegan bought some land near Goudhurst in Kent, and using Canadian-style barns and equipment, started training boys for Farming in Canada, but it does seem that the length of the training given was rather varied, and also that boys were sent "to make up the number of the party" even though their training was not completed.

One Old Fegan boy, who later became a qualified Minister of a number of Churches in Canada, told me himself that he only spent two weeks at the Training Farm before being sent to Canada, which was very unfair to himself-and his future employer.

Much has been written recently about children (not Fegan boys) who were sent to countries, such as Canada and Australia, to help build the Empire, and a recent Television documentary about orphan children being sent to Australia in the 1950s was really horrific.

There is no doubt that Mr. Fegan's intentions were to give his boys who were orphaned, homeless, or just simply unwanted, a new start in life when the opportunities of this Country were rather limited. He also set up a Receiving Home in Canada and installed a member of his Staff and his wife to accommodate the boys on their arrival and to place them in jobs with Farmers and also to visit them from time to time and keep in touch with them, offering any help or advice that was needed.

I suppose the best thing is for me to print an article written by Richard Wright, a boy who went to Canada in 1938, and let him tell his own story.

RECOLLECTIONS OF A FEGAN BOY ON MIGRATING TO CANADA IN 1938

How exciting! I had been chosen to migrate to Canada with fifteen other boys. Canada? Eskimos, Indians, wide open prairies, log houses, no conveniences. No! Fegan boys were much better informed. Many of the misconceptions of the time were not part of a Fegan boy's idea of this great land. I well remember the photographs of Canada hanging on dormitory walls at Goudhurst. Some, to be sure, of reaping on the prairies, Indian camps, haying scenes. But, also pictures of modern farming methods, beautiful cities like Toronto, Montreal, Calgary and Vancouver.

I knew this was going to be a wonderful adventure, and I was going to be a big farmer, perhaps even a rancher with cowboys, real ones, working for me!

How can one forget the preparations. Mr. Walmsley's somewhat exaggerated imitation of a Canadian accent, the traffic in Toronto, and how we should always do as the "Missus" told us when we arrived at our job. Then the outfitting . . . all those shirts, two dress suits, six huge handkerchiefs, plimsolls, work boots, etc. etc. etc. The huge trunk (my Son has it now) and the packing instructions we followed so carefully. After over fifty years of hiving off boys to Canada, Fegans really knew how!!! It would cost a month's salary to buy that trunk full of clothes today.

April 8, 1938, was a cold, rather dull morning and after sleeping rather fitfully, I was somewhat numb mentally when I climbed out of bed and into the bath, cleaned my teeth and donned one of those lovely suits. Mine was brown with a little pin stripe. Then a quick breakfast and the trip to Marden to board the train for London. No problem for our masters though. We were young gentlemen, going to build the great British Empire, so we behaved perfectly. No pushing and shoving, just young men boarding the train on our way to making our mark in the world! After changing trains at Euston, I believe, we travelled on what appeared to be a very slow train to Liverpool. I could not wait to see that great Liner, the Duchess of Bedford, and walk up the gangplank. We would soon be off on the great adventure to a far off land we had only read about in our geography books! Thoughts raced through my mind as the train rumbled along through the beautiful English countryside. Little did I realise how long it would be until I travelled that same line again and watch the yellow gorse flashing by and the back gardens of the houses passing with but a glimpse.

The Old Duchess was a beautiful ship and everyone was so hospitable. Our steward called us "sir", as did our waiter at meal times. No more saluting masters (oh, how I hated that). We were shown to our cabins, with two boys in a cabin, one bunk over the other. I was in a cabin with

Ronald Warren. I often wondered what happened to him, as we were friends when we were at Stony.

We spent ten wonderful days on this great Canadian Pacific Liner. Nothing but fun, very little regimentation, spoiled only by that horrible sea-sickness. I wished I would die, and I am sure I nearly did.

Mr. Smith, the Homes deputation secretary, had the onerous task of leading the party to Canada. We must have driven him to distraction, making sure we were all in our bunks at the appointed time, leading us at prayers, making sure we were clean and well dressed. To lead fifteen boys on a 3000 mile trip across the ocean must have been quite a task.

I remember a couple of days out on the Atlantic, a few of us were playing football on the stern deck and guess who kicked the ball overboard? I truly thought the rest of the boys were going to throw me overboard to get the ball. I wonder who owned that football?

We sailed up the St. Lawrence River and dropped anchor at Quebec City. I remember how poor it looked. Fifty years later I realised what I thought was a poverty stricken village, was the old city of Quebec, built over 300 years ago by the early settlers of Canada.

At Quebec, Mr. W. J. Hutchinson came on board to lead us on to Toronto, and to facilitate our landed immigrant status. Incidentally, there was no such thing as a Canadian citizen in those days. We were all British subjects with all the rights and privileges of a Canadian as soon as we landed at Montreal. Canadians we would soon become, proud of our Country. In fact, some of us died for Canada in the second World War. I can assure you it did not take me long to become very Canadian, including acquiring a Canadian accent, enjoying Canadian food, and best of all, marrying a beautiful Canadian girl after some seven years in Canada. I can even pronounce our great Ontario city so that native Canadians can understand. Over here we call it Tronna, you know.

There is one thing I shall always remember about our trip across the ocean and up the mighty St. Lawrence River to Montreal. After Uncle Hutch came on board, it did not take him long to discover the organ in the third class lounge. Uncle Hutch was the organist at Jarvis Street Baptist Church, the great Church in Toronto that stood firm for the truth of the Bible over the years. As Fegan boys we could sing. Most of us had sung in the choir and Mrs. E. O. Swell, the wife of our Headmaster at Stony Stratford, had taught us how to read music, for which I will always be grateful. Between Mr. Smith and Uncle Hutch, they rounded us up (the old Duchess was a big ship) and gathered us around the organ, gave us a hymn book and we sang to the passengers in the lounge. The room was full of smoke. It seemed everyone smoked in those days. Some were playing cards. Others were gambling, throwing two huge dice on the floor. I don't think anyone was interested in a group of young teenage boys singing gospel hymns at ten o'clock in the morning. Gradually, as we sang, one number after another, the cards lay still on the tables, the dice no longer clattered on the floor, the smoke started to thin and the beer was left in the glass as the room became silent, but for the sound of our voices. One of the hymns we sang was "When the Roll is Called Up Yonder" and one elderly gentleman with a huge cigar in his hand started to sob. We boys, who were not too enthused about singing to a group of strangers in a smoke filled room, became quite subdued. The man came to talk to Uncle Hutch after our impromptu concert and unburdened his heart, telling Uncle Hutch he was brought up on the prairies by a God-fearing mother and father, but had not listened to them and now after many years the old hymn had reminded him that he needed to turn his life to Jesus Christ, so that "When the Roll is called up yonder, he would be there with mum and dad!"

Finally, after a very slow trip up the river, we arrived at Montreal and walked down the gangplank and put our feet on Canadian soil. I can still remember the thrill, and yet the bittersweet feeling of homesickness, and perhaps a little fear of the unknown. It was then, I think, I finally realised the enormity of the decision I had made some three months before, when I applied to come to Canada. You see, my children are Canadians by birth. I am proud to be a Canadian by choice. However, the mixed emotions soon disappeared in the excitement of finding my trunk and making sure it was on its way to the Montreal railway station. Then we were all jammed into taxis (I think) and driven to the station to board the train for Toronto. The only thing I remember about that journey from Montreal to Toronto was how slow the train travelled. In Britain the trains travel at quite high speeds. Slower the Canadian Pacific train may have been, but this was my first practical lesson in the great distance we travel in Canada between cities. It is much further from Montreal to Toronto than it is from London to Edinburgh.

The Receiving Home at 247 Broadview Avenue, Toronto, Canada.

Then three wonderful days at the Fegan receiving home in Toronto at 247 Broadview Avenue. It was a big house on a corner which doubled as a residence for Mr. Hutchinson and accommodation for a party of fifteen or twenty boys. There, once again, Mr. Fegan's Homes showed the great love and dedication they had to us boys. This was three days of enjoyment and orientation to help us adapt to life in Canada. Swimming at the Broadview Y.M.C.A. – in the nude I might add – good food cooked by Mrs. Hutchinson and a limousine tour of the city of Toronto, compliments of one of the large dealerships in the city. Mr. Hutchinson explained what life would be like on an Ontario farm, how we should conduct ourselves when living in the farmer's home, the importance of kindness to animals and even a lesson about sex.

Wednesday morning, April 21, dawned clear and quite warm, unusually warm for this time of year. This was the big day I had been looking forward to – my first job in Canada! What would my new boss be like? What did an Ontario farm look like? What would my first job be?

There was a feeling of expectancy and yet apprehension, perhaps even fear. I boarded the train at Union Station Toronto for Aurora, Ontario, a town so close to Toronto, perhaps twenty-five miles away, it is now almost part of the city.

I was met at the station by a thin, stooped, old gentleman, who saw me sitting on my trunk on the station platform. After asking my name, he identified himself as Mr. Frank Graham, shook my hand and said "You are my man", and proceeded to help me with my trunk. Outside the station stood an ancient automobile of nondescript colour. It was a 1927 Whippet, manufactured by the Willys company, the designer of the famous "Jeep" of the second World War. I was used to the usual method of shopping. You produced money, the merchant supplied goods. Now I am in Canada among the pioneers. Mr. Graham stopped at the General Store on Wellington Street in Aurora, removed a large bag from the rear seat of the car and we both marched into the store. Mr. Graham then proceeded to remove some large Spanish onions and the most beautiful brown eggs from the bag and bartered them for various grocery items. Now I knew I was in Canada, where perhaps they didn't use money. Not a penny changed hands. In fact, as I remember I did not see a cash register. Of course I was soon to find out that money was very necessary in Canada. In fact, my salary for the first year on the farm was seventy-five dollars per year and my board and lodging.

Mr. Graham lived about three and a half miles from

town on a dirt road. I hadnot seen a dirt road in England and it was strange to look out of the rear window of the car and see nothing but clouds of dust. Mr. Graham was a very kindly Christian man, but he was dying. He had cancer of the liver and was only fifty seven years old. He died in July of 1938 and I sang "The way of the Cross Leads Home" at his funeral.

I soon adapted to Canadian life, became an active member of an evangelical Church, and only once did I succumb to homesickness. One cold damp day in May I was in the silo forking silage out for the cattle and I remember sticking the fork in the silage and, leaning the handle against the wall of the silo, sitting on the handle and crying my eyes out. Loneliness can be the worst human emotion, but I thank the Lord that He was at my side at all times to "bind the broken hearted".

I shall ever be thankful for the circumstances that put me in Fegan's in the first place, and to Fegans for giving me the opportunity to migrate to this Wonderful Land.

Chapter Twelve

Finale

This has basically been a story about myself and my experiences as a boy, the time spent in Mr. Fegan's Homes and about some of the people (mainly boys and Staff) whom I have met and lived with, and yet there is so much that could still be written about the work of Mr. Fegan and his boys.

There are thousands of boys who have passed through the Homes and, of course, they could all write similar stories, as Richard Wright has done.

The number on the Boys Outfit List, in a previous chapter, put me as No. 5449. That may well not go back to the beginning of Mr. Fegan's work and it certainly wasn't the end of it. However, it does give some idea of the number of boys that have been given a home and shelter by those who gave their lives to this great work.

I once went to Earls Court to hear Billy Graham preach, and, while we waited for the service to begin, the man next to me, who was a complete stranger, talked to me and told me he came from a big family, of which he was very proud. After some time of telling me about his family, he then said to me "Do you come from a big family?" and I said "Oh, yes". "How many in your family?" he asked, and, as casually as I could, I said "Oh, about 180".

Like all families it had it's faults and short-comings. There were some things that should never have happened. Some eras that were better than others, and, of course, in an ideal world there should not have been a need for Homes for boys and girls, but I know I am not alone when I say that, despite it's many failings, I believe that the work of Mr. Fegan's Homes was unique. I am proud to be a member of this family whose motives have always been to help boys (and later girls) in need and now, in the present day, whole families.

Author standing outside the door he entered when arriving as a boy in 1944.

A number of years ago, after I had left Fegan's, I was travelling in a coach to the Westminster Central Hall, where Fegan's Homes were holding their Annual Meeting and Display. Unfortunately, "Ban the Bomb" protesters were sitting down in most of the roads leading into the city and thus blocking the way in. After almost despairing of reaching our destination, the coach-driver managed to drive past Buckingham Palace, into Birdcage Walk and turning right into a side Street, pulled up outside the Central Hall. Immediately two Policemen pounced on our coach, pulled the door open, and looking at me, as the nearest passenger, one of them said "Alright, and who are you lot?" I told him that we were a group of people going to Mr. Fegan's Homes' Annual Meeting at the Central Hall and he turned to his colleague and said "Fegan's Homes? 'Cor, we get 'em all up 'ere, don't we!"

Perhaps many people in this Country have never heard of Mr. Fegan, or his Homes, so maybe what I have written will give the Reader an insight into this Great Man and his work. And to the lady who wrote and asked me what it was really like in the Home, as a boy, I trust that I have been able to paint a true picture.

Maybe I could summarise all this in a short poem I have written, and most boys who were at Stony Stratford and Goudhurst will see themselves in it somewhere.

The Finale

Were You There?

Were you there at Stony Stratford and called a Fegan kid
Where the Staff seemed ever watchful of everything you did?
Did you scrub the tiled passage or line beds up in the Dorm
And play penny-on-the-wicket to a batsman out of form?
Can you remember, in the Chapel, listening to 'Happy Jim'
Or were you in the Choir where Dad Swell taught you to sing?
Did you play in Fegan's colours in stripes of black and red
Or were you caught at scrumping apples and promptly sent to bed?
Did you ever climb the steeple, not concerned that you might fall
Or walk round the Chapel gutter to get your tennis ball?
There are so many things to mention that time does not allow
Like when we let the pigs out and how we tried to catch the sow.
Did you ever go to Goudhurst when you'd left the Stony School
And run home from apple-picking for a quick dip in the pool?
Did you work with cows and horses or maybe with the sheep
Or help bring in the harvest with corn and oats to reap?
Did you worship in the Chapel and maybe give a sigh
When Gipsy Williams' daughter sang and brought a tear into your eye?
Alas, those days have gone for ever and life will never be the same
So may I thank you Mr. Fegan for the memories that remain.

Written by   S.A.S.   22.4.1994.